CHARTREUSE LIGHT

-Beyond the Boundary Fanbook-

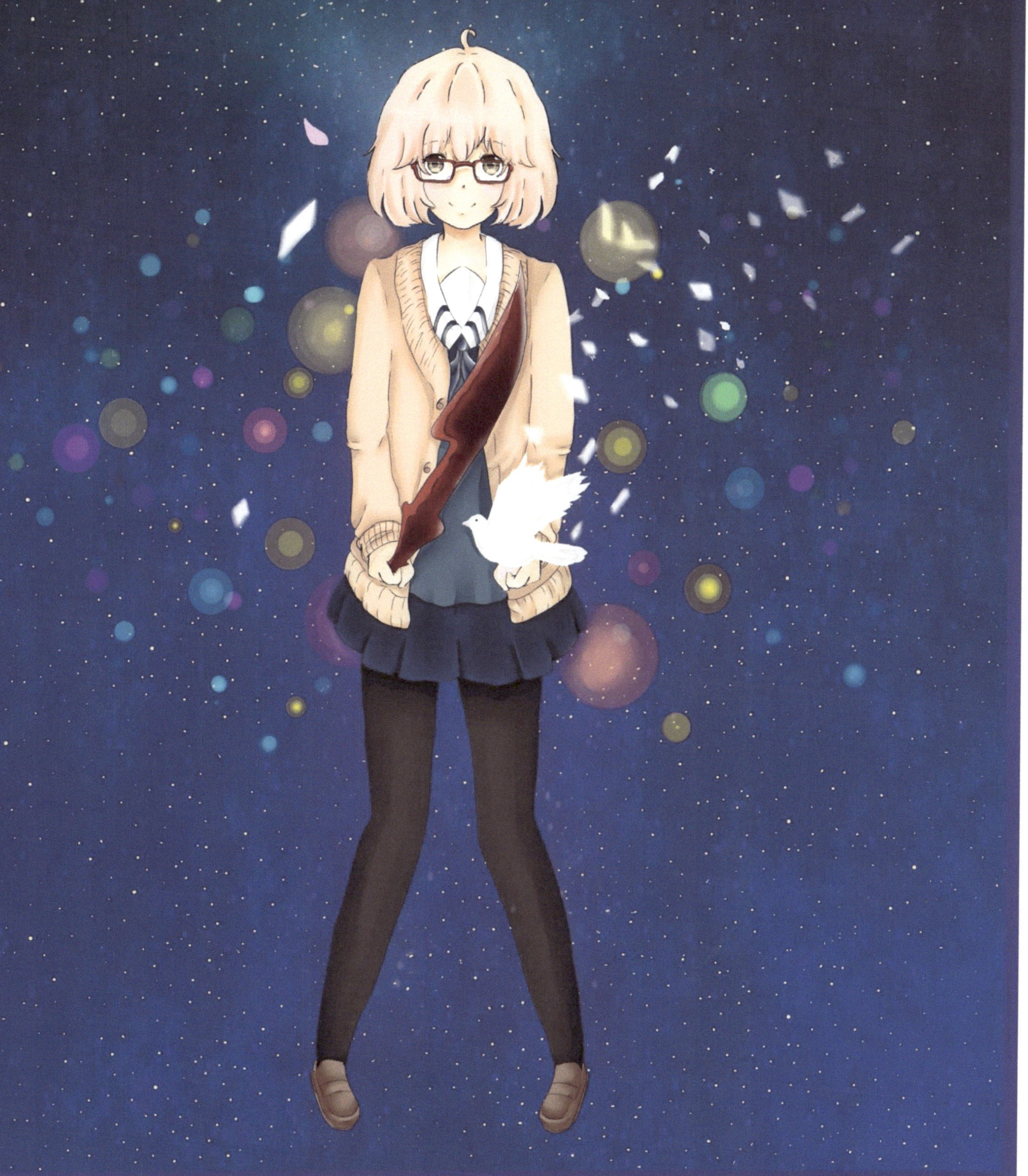

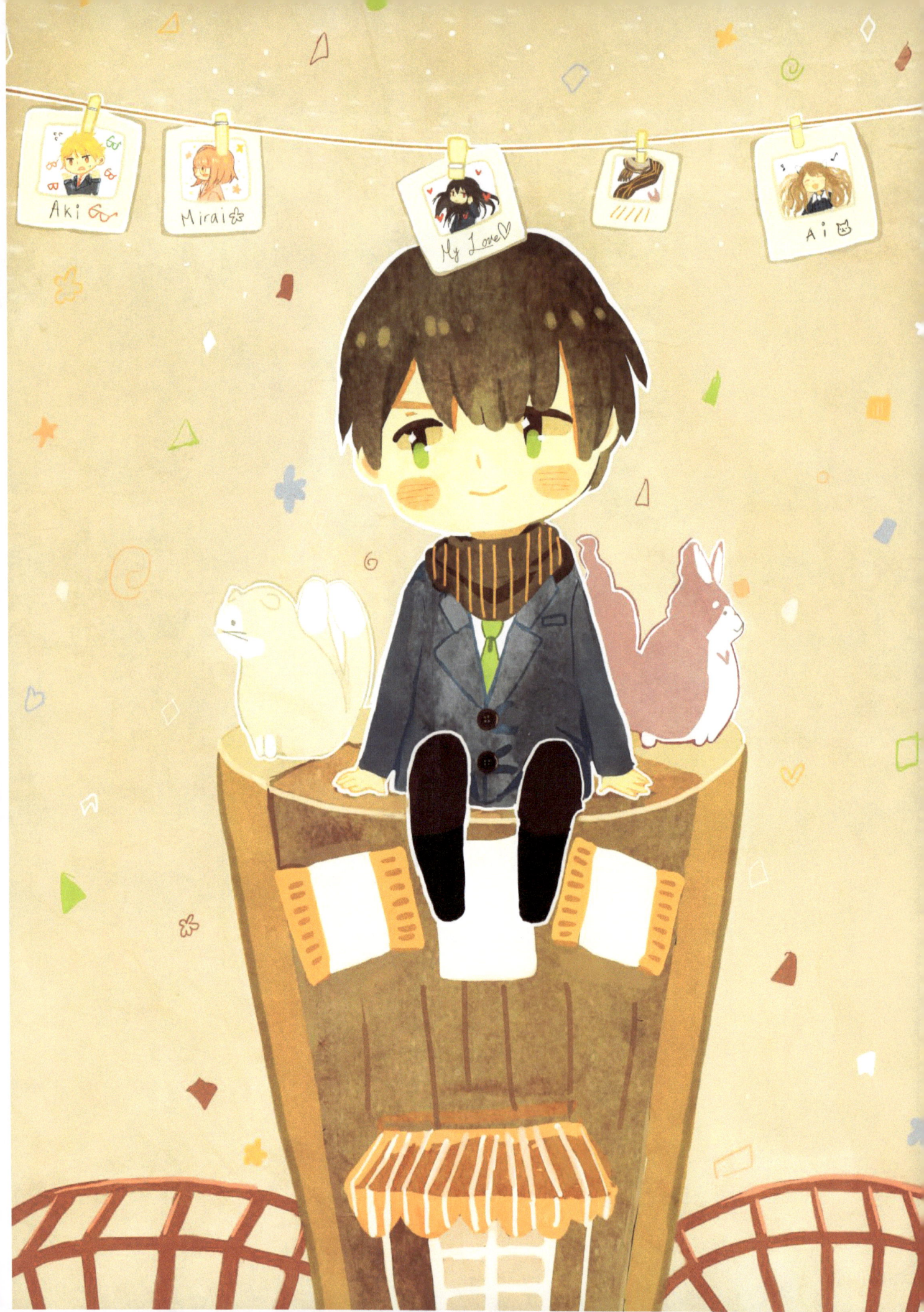

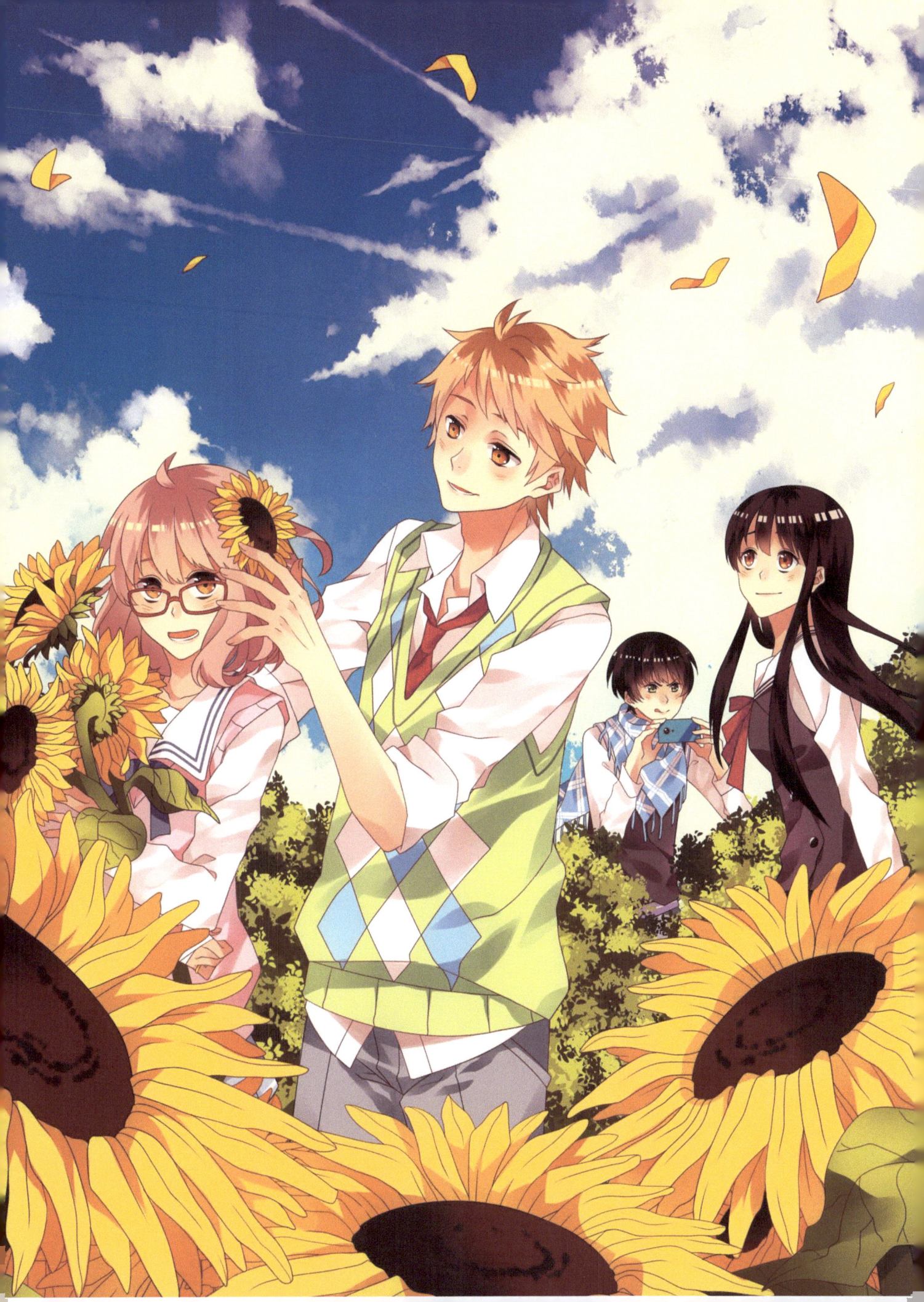

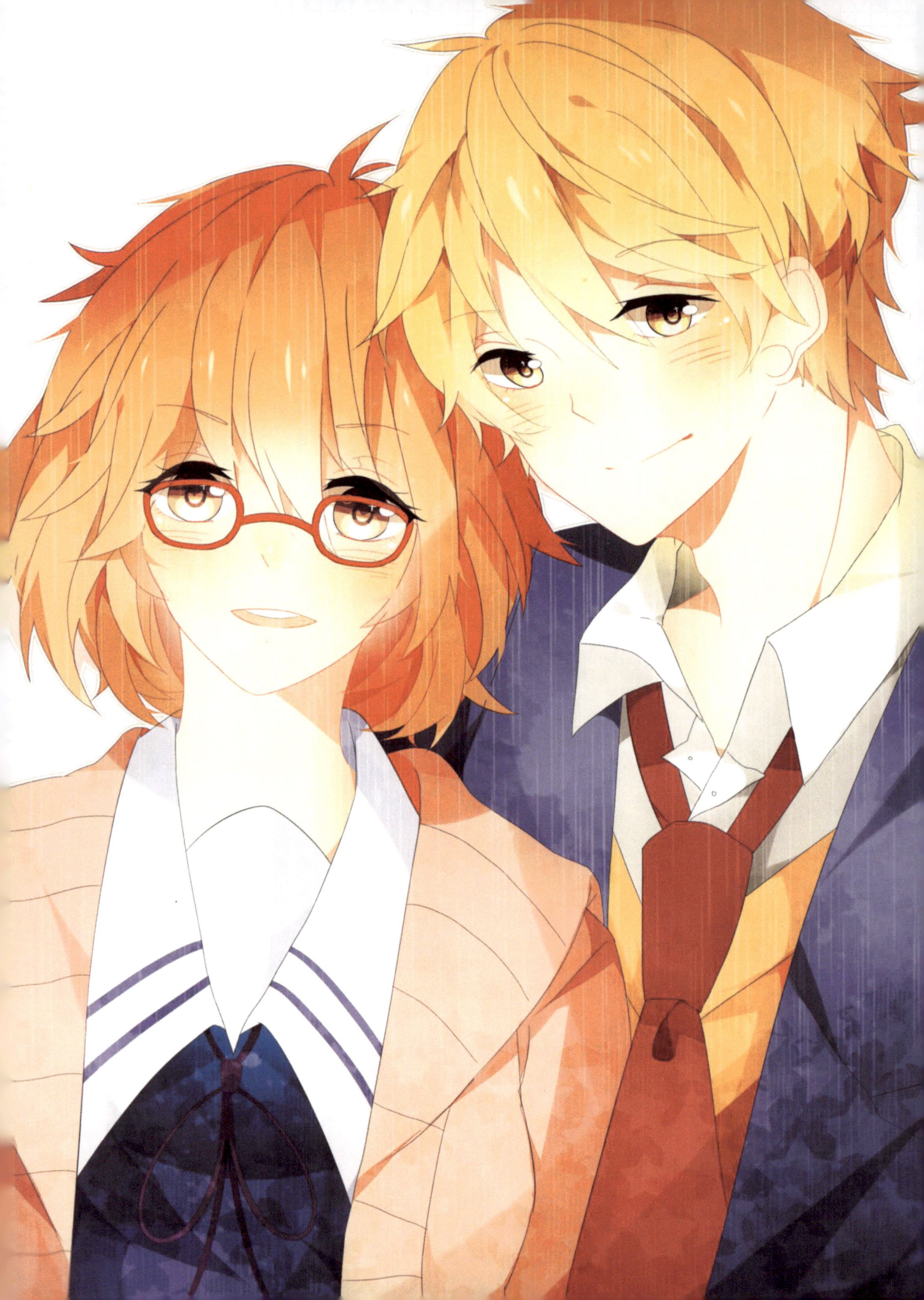

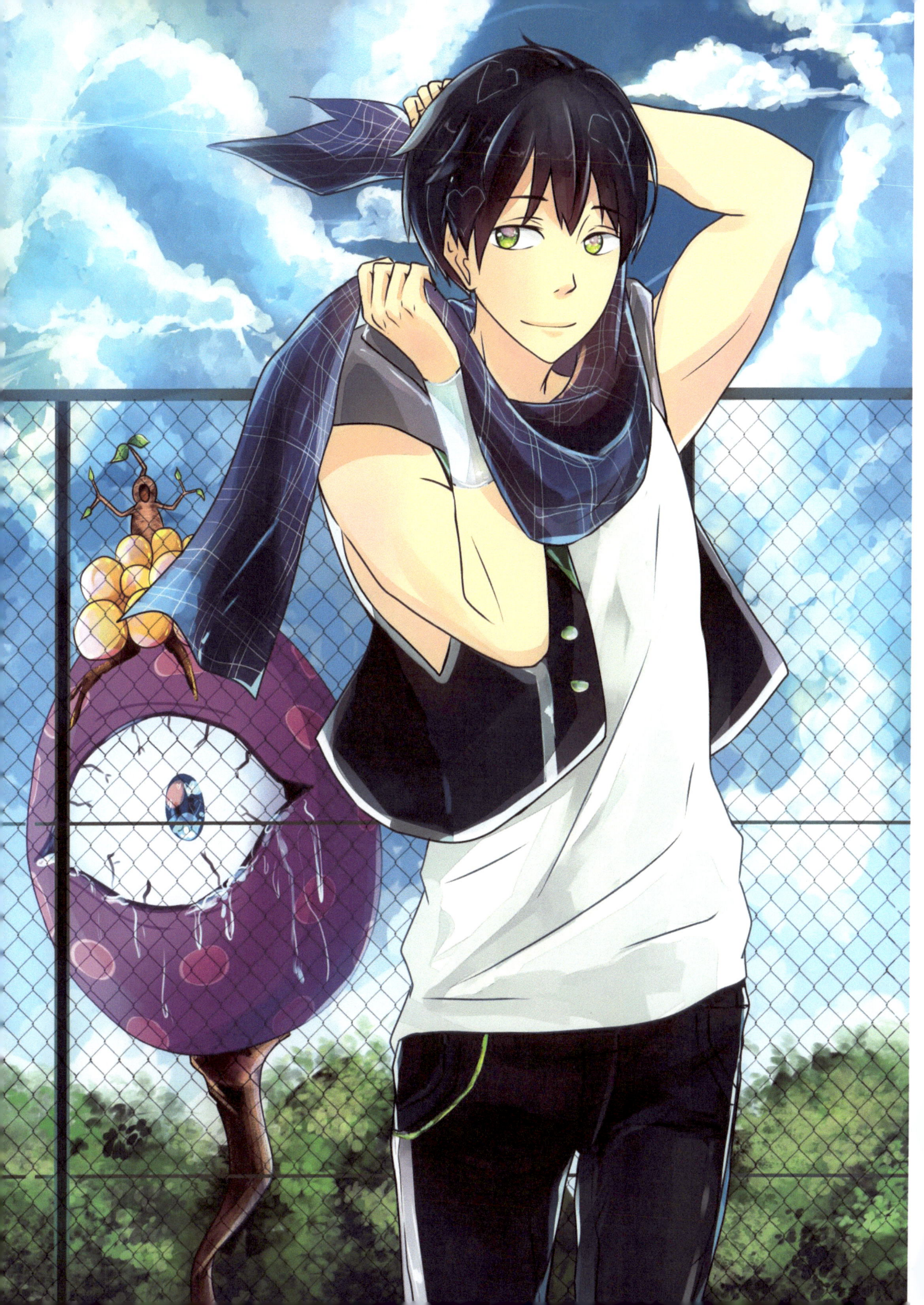

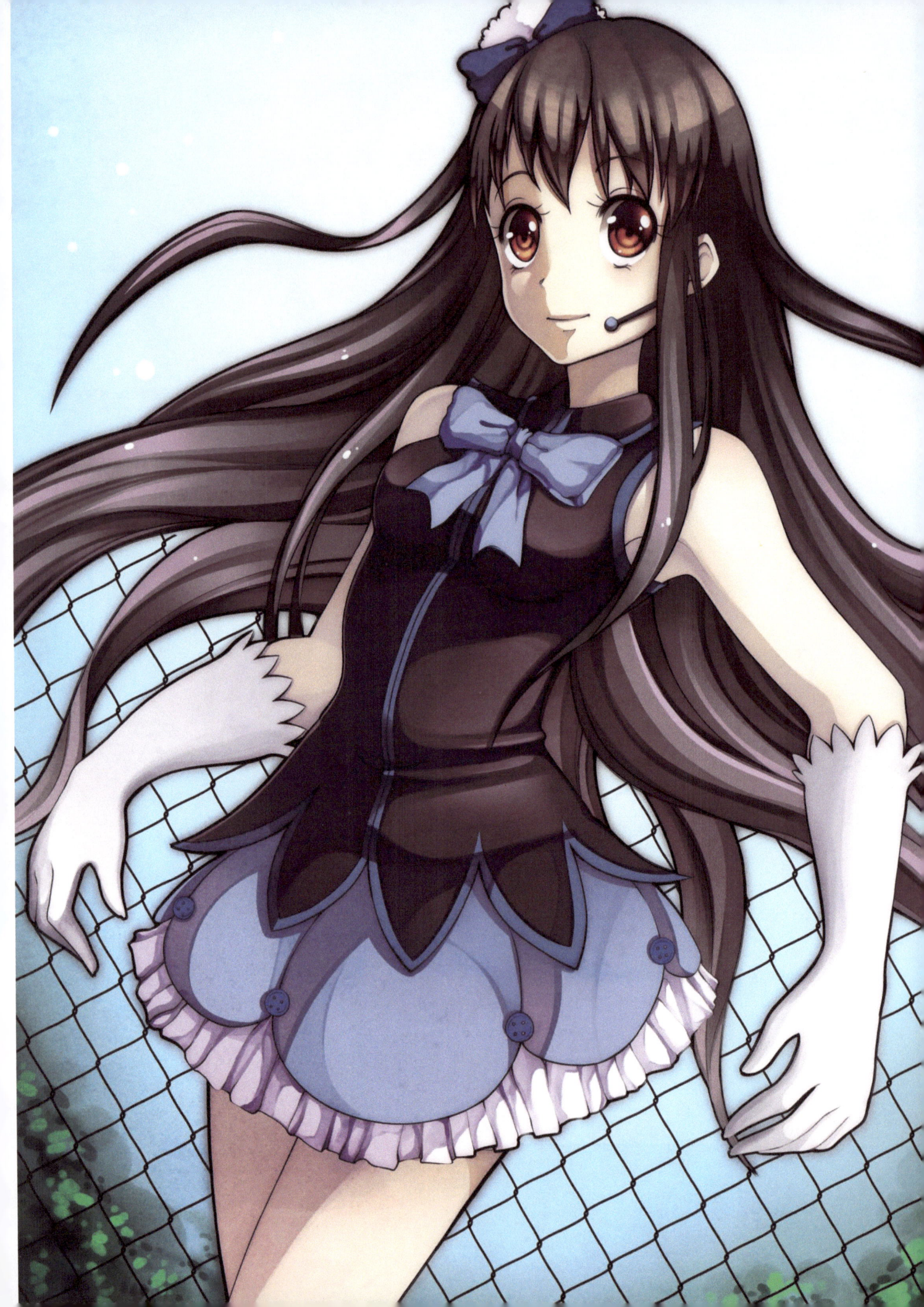

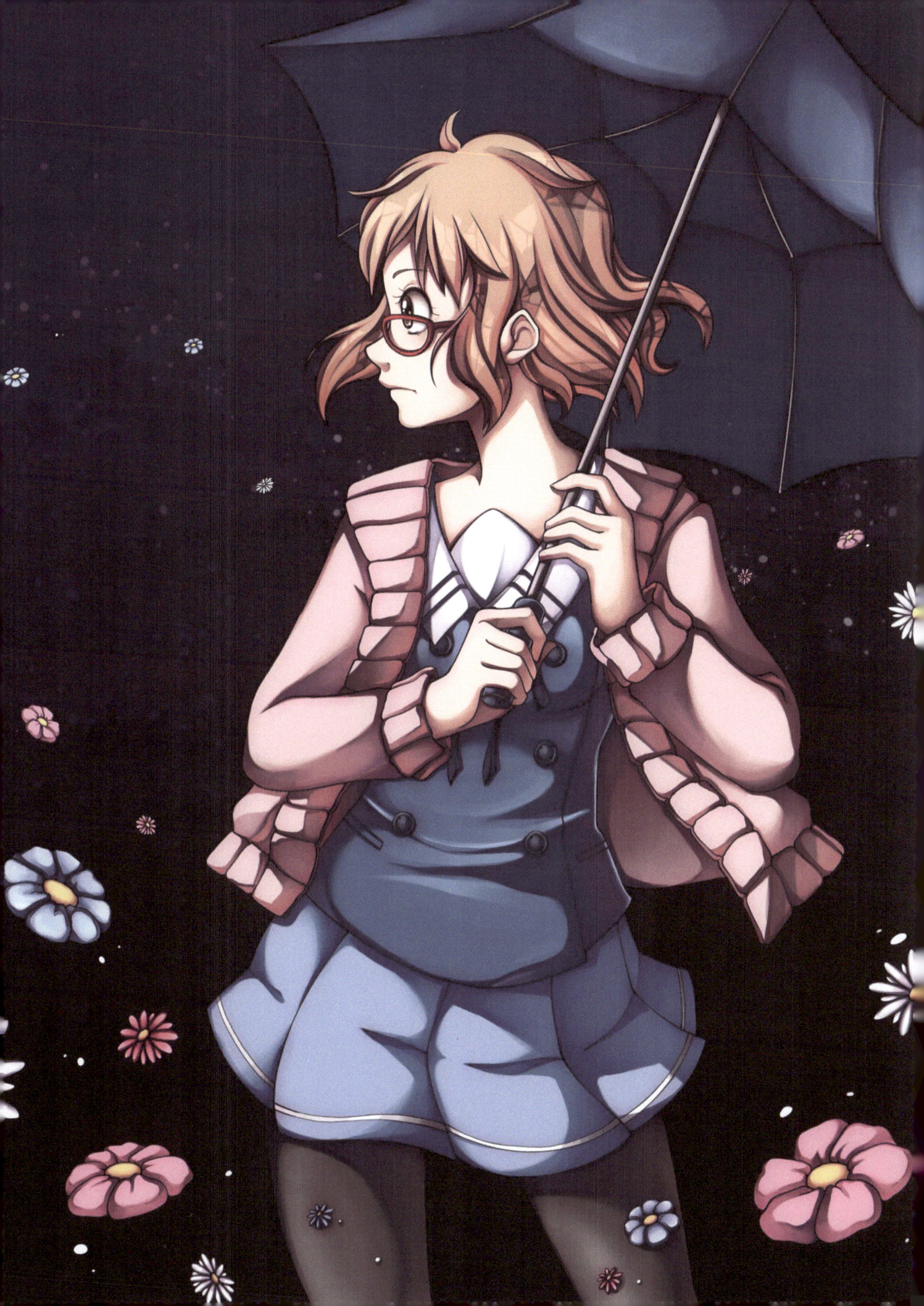

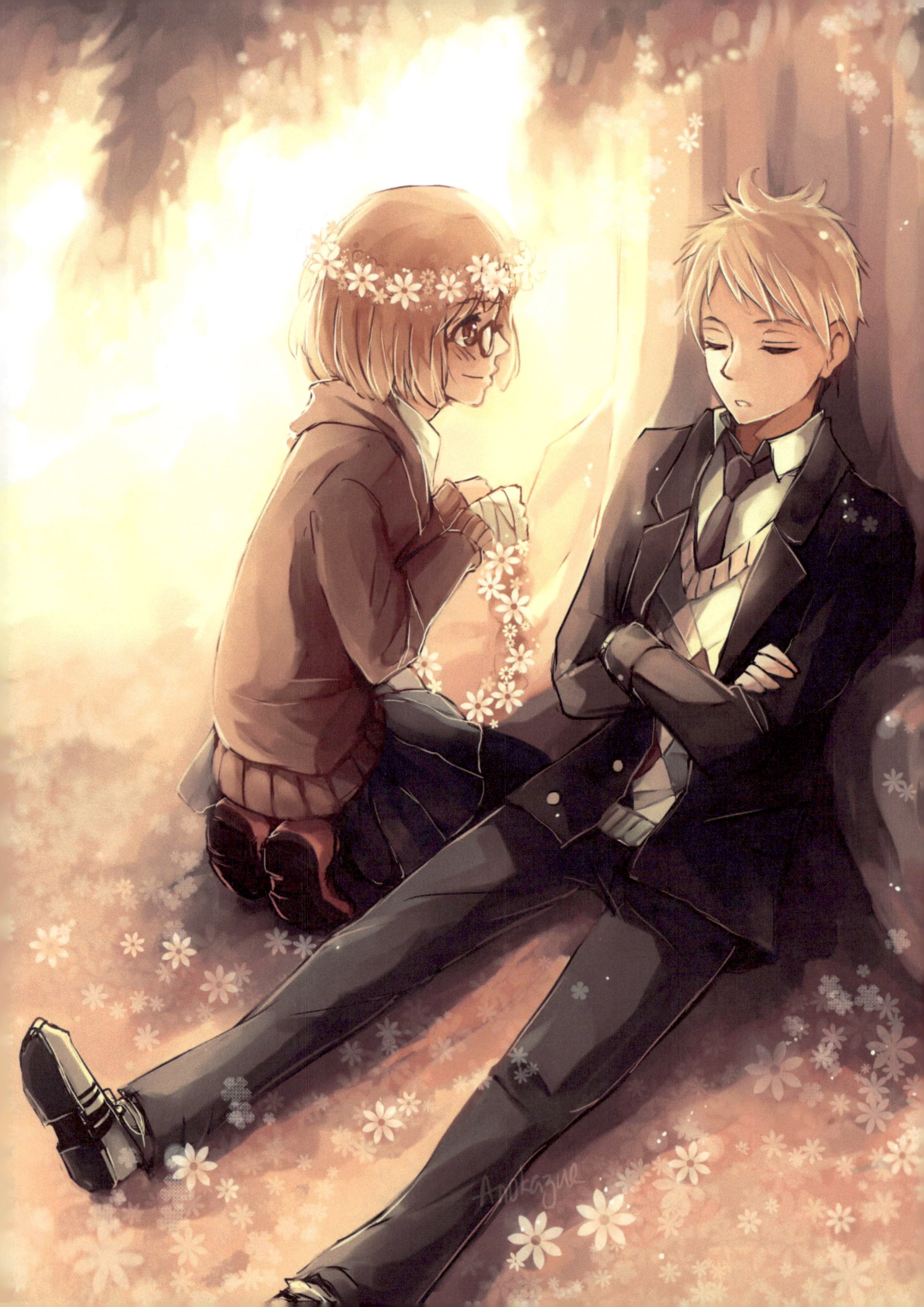

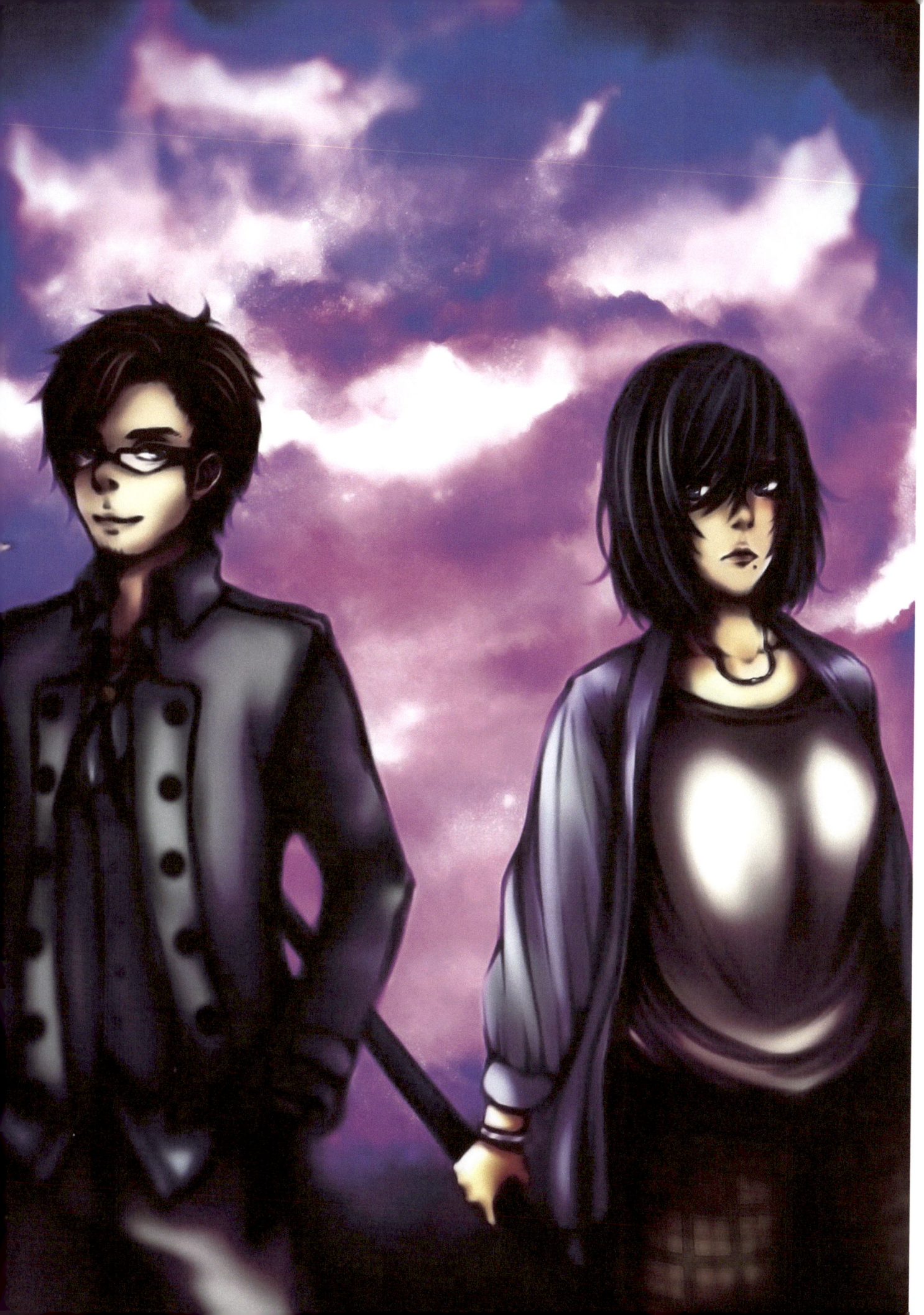

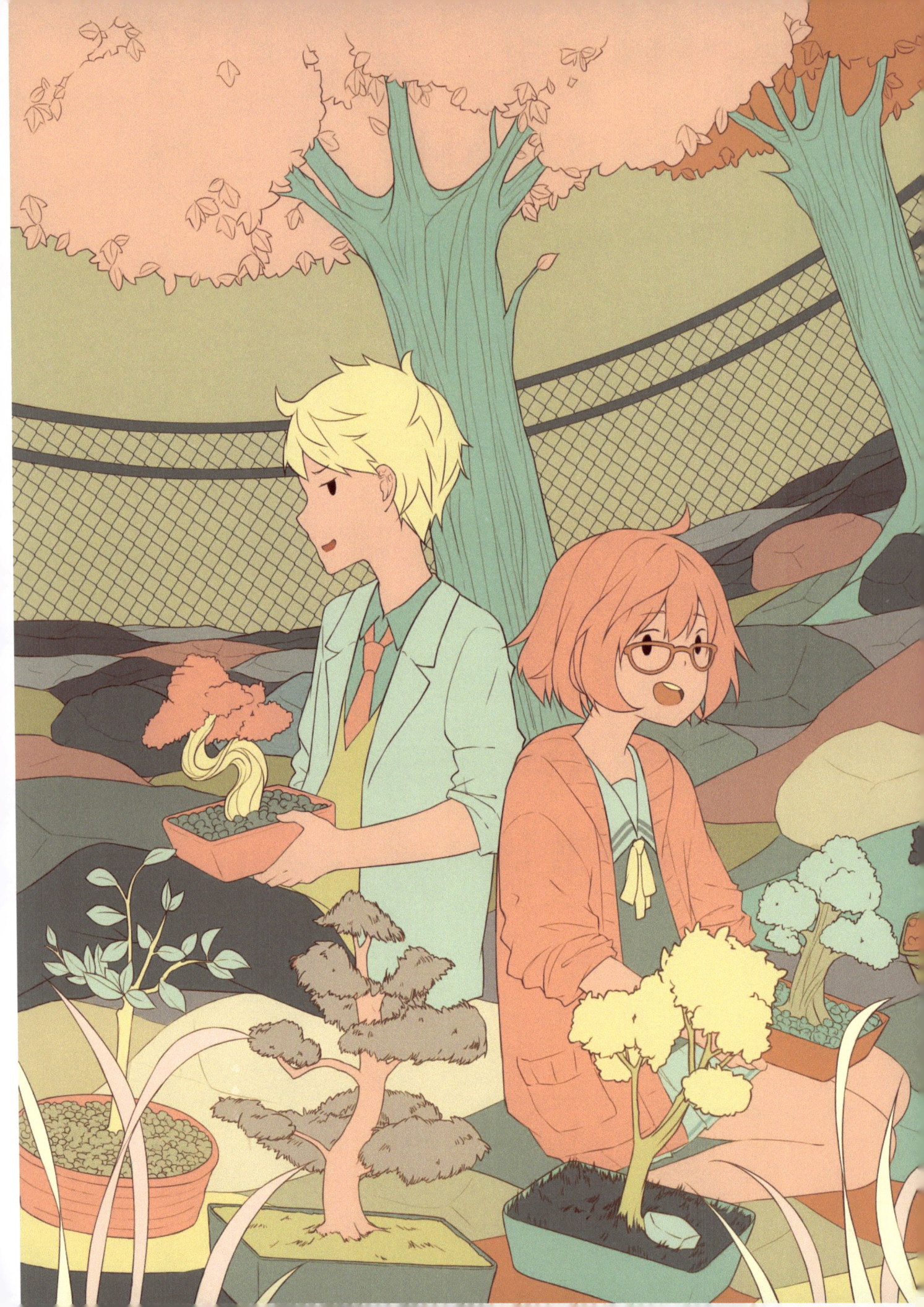

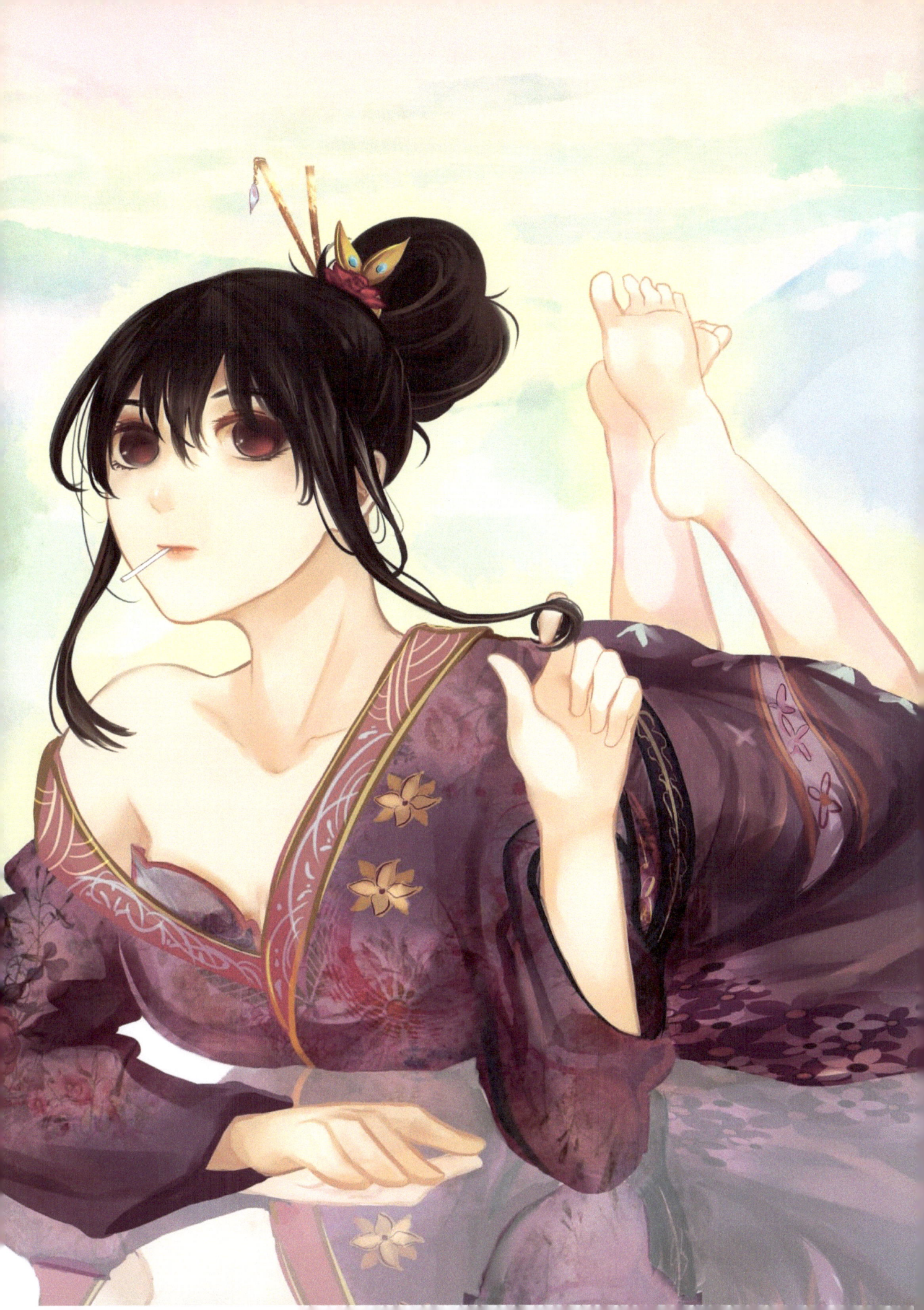

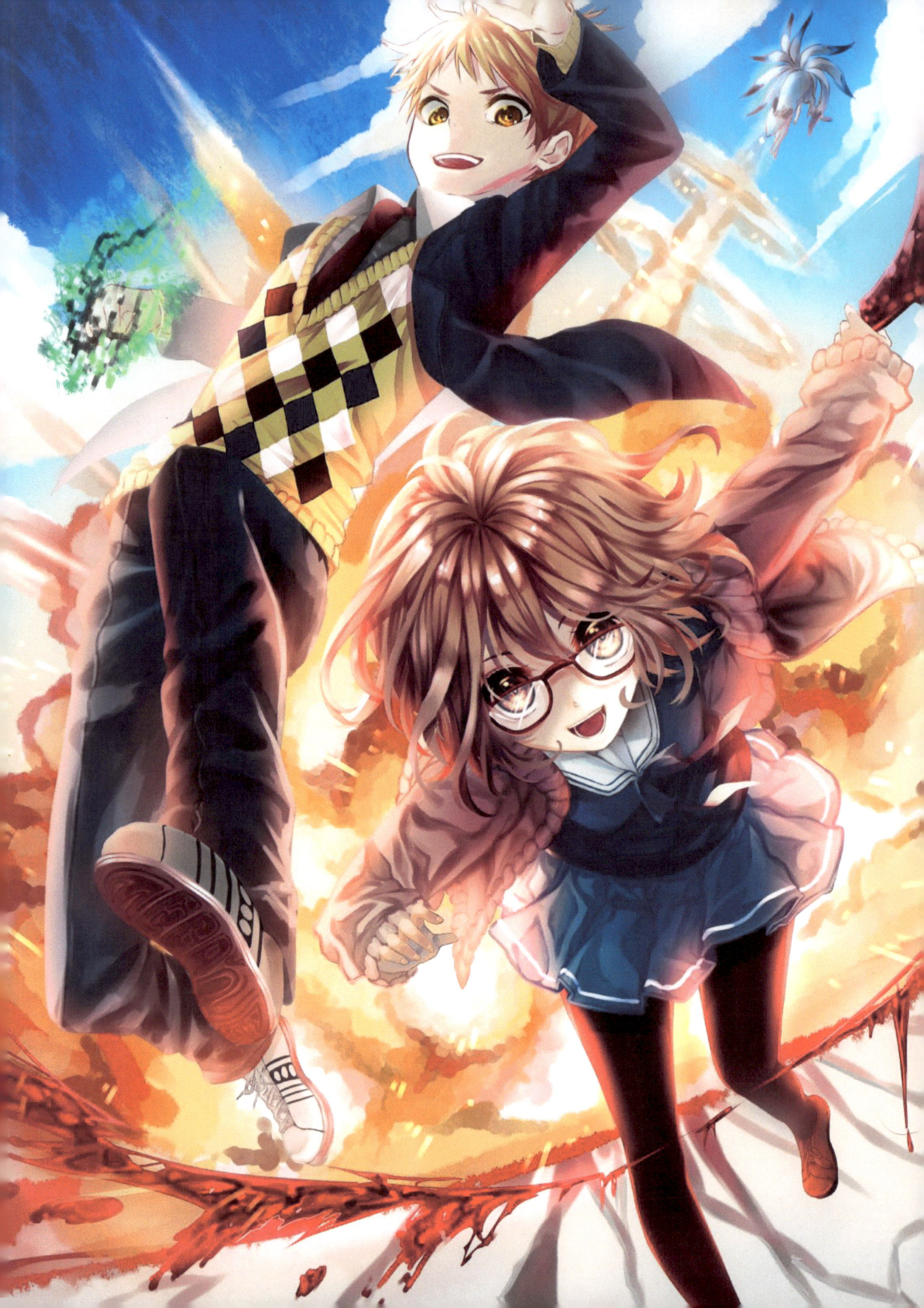

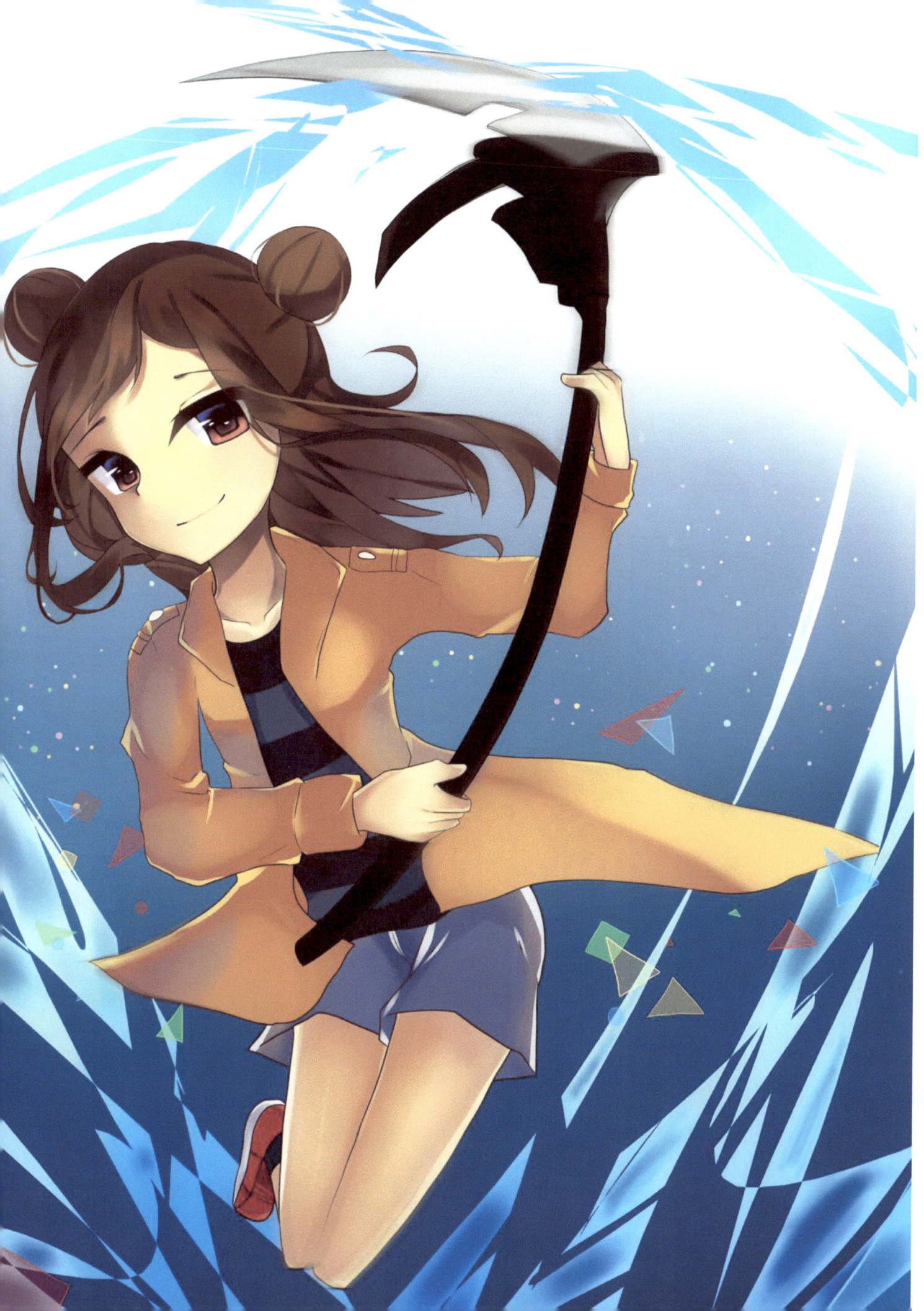

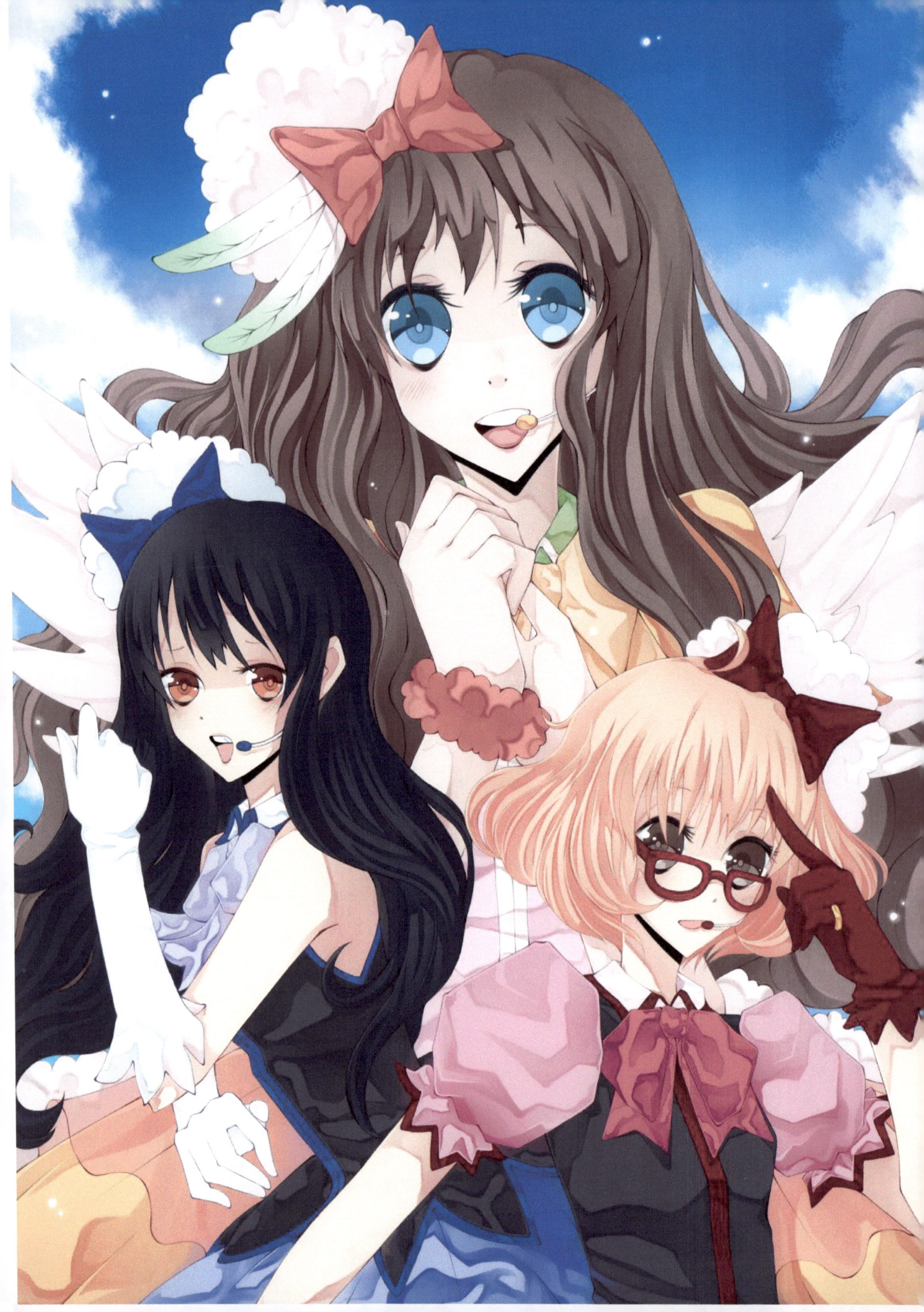

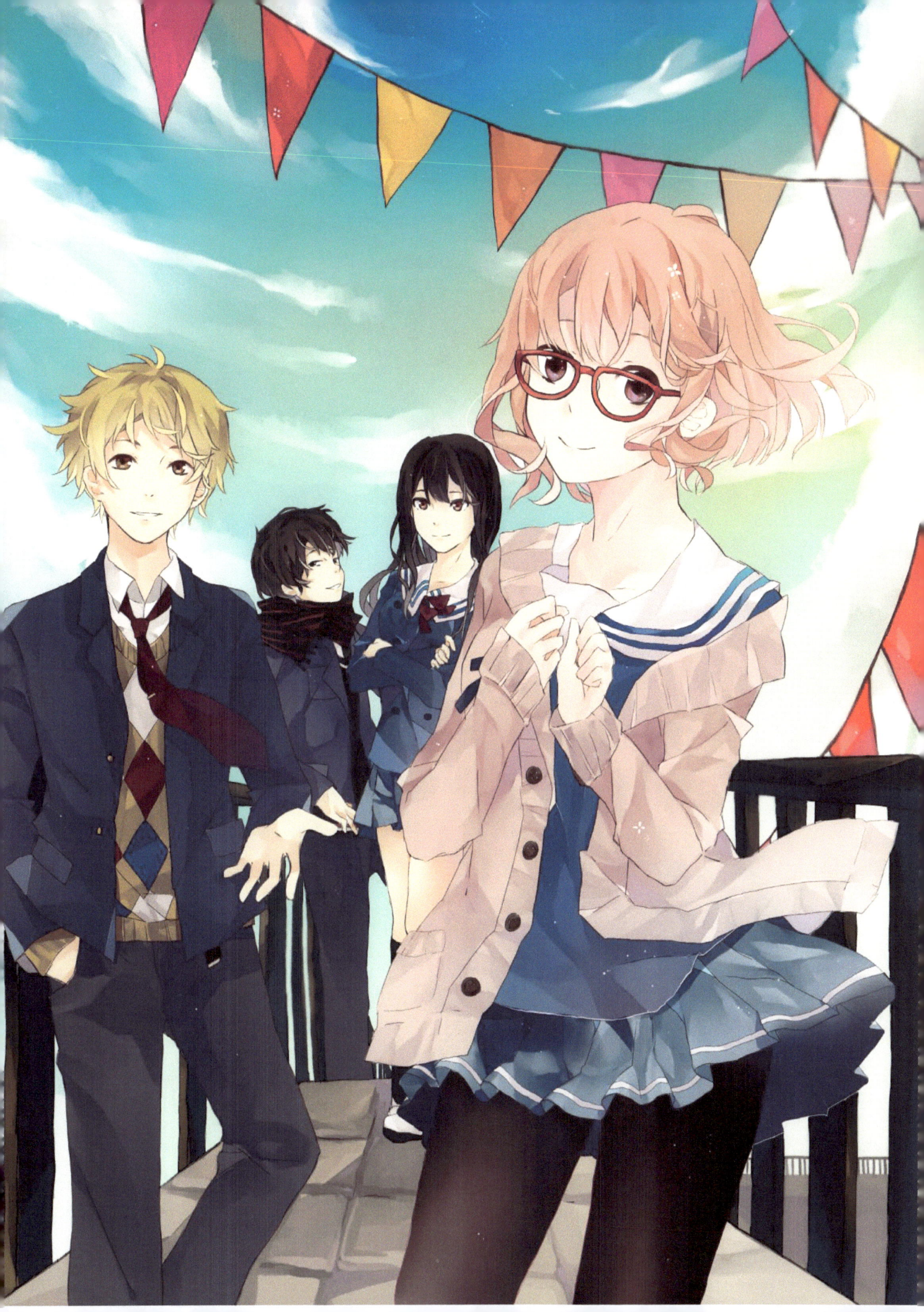

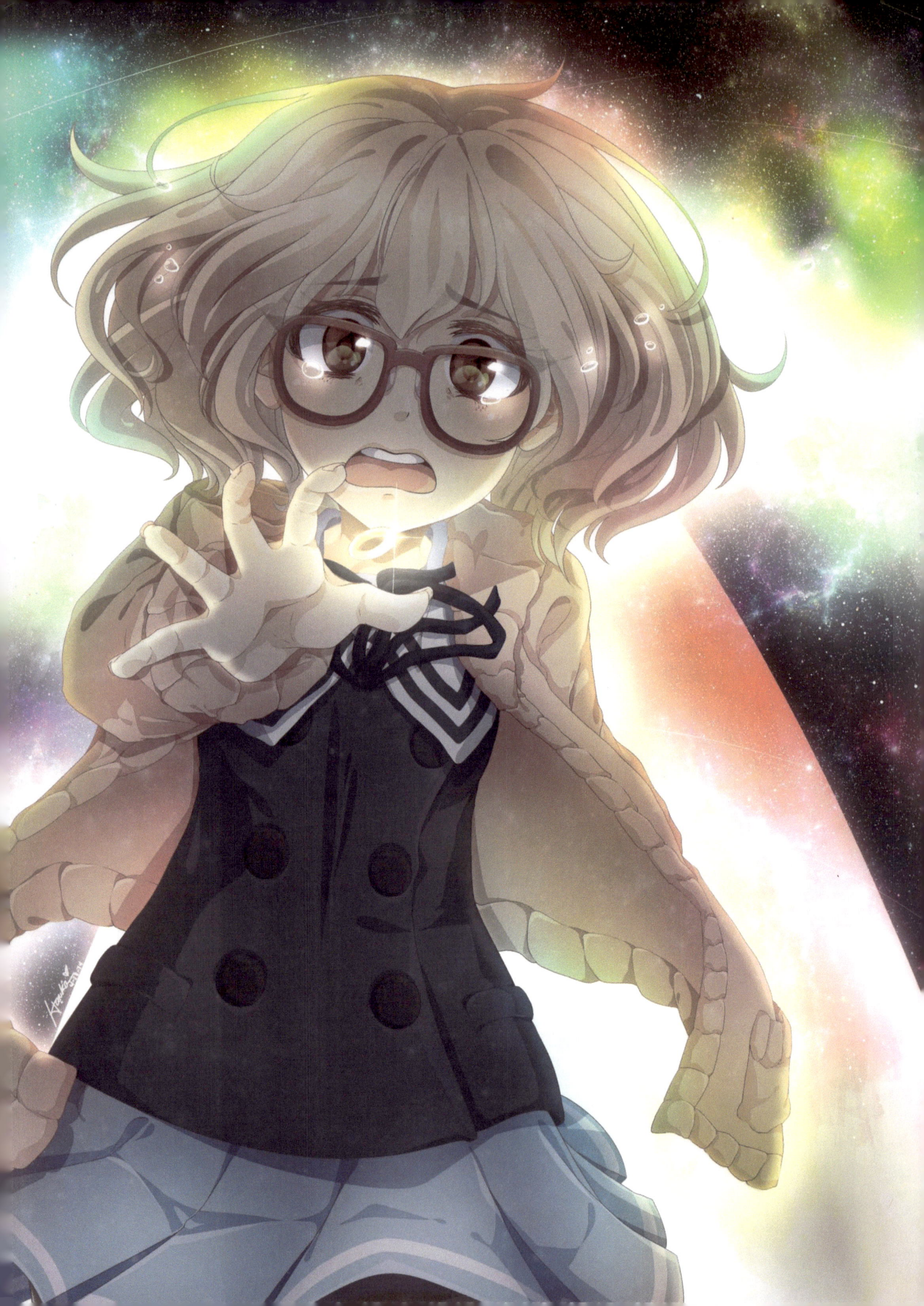

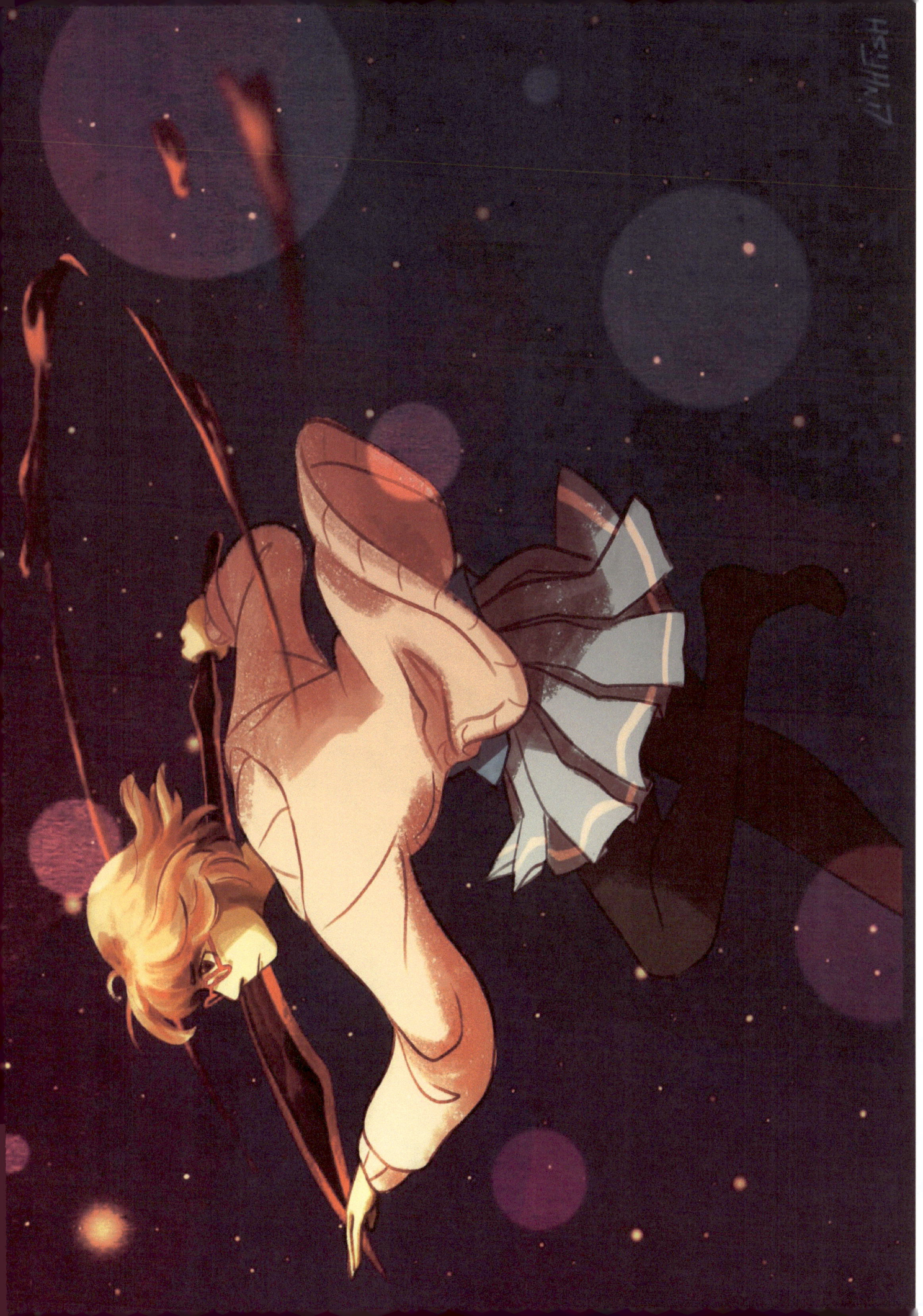

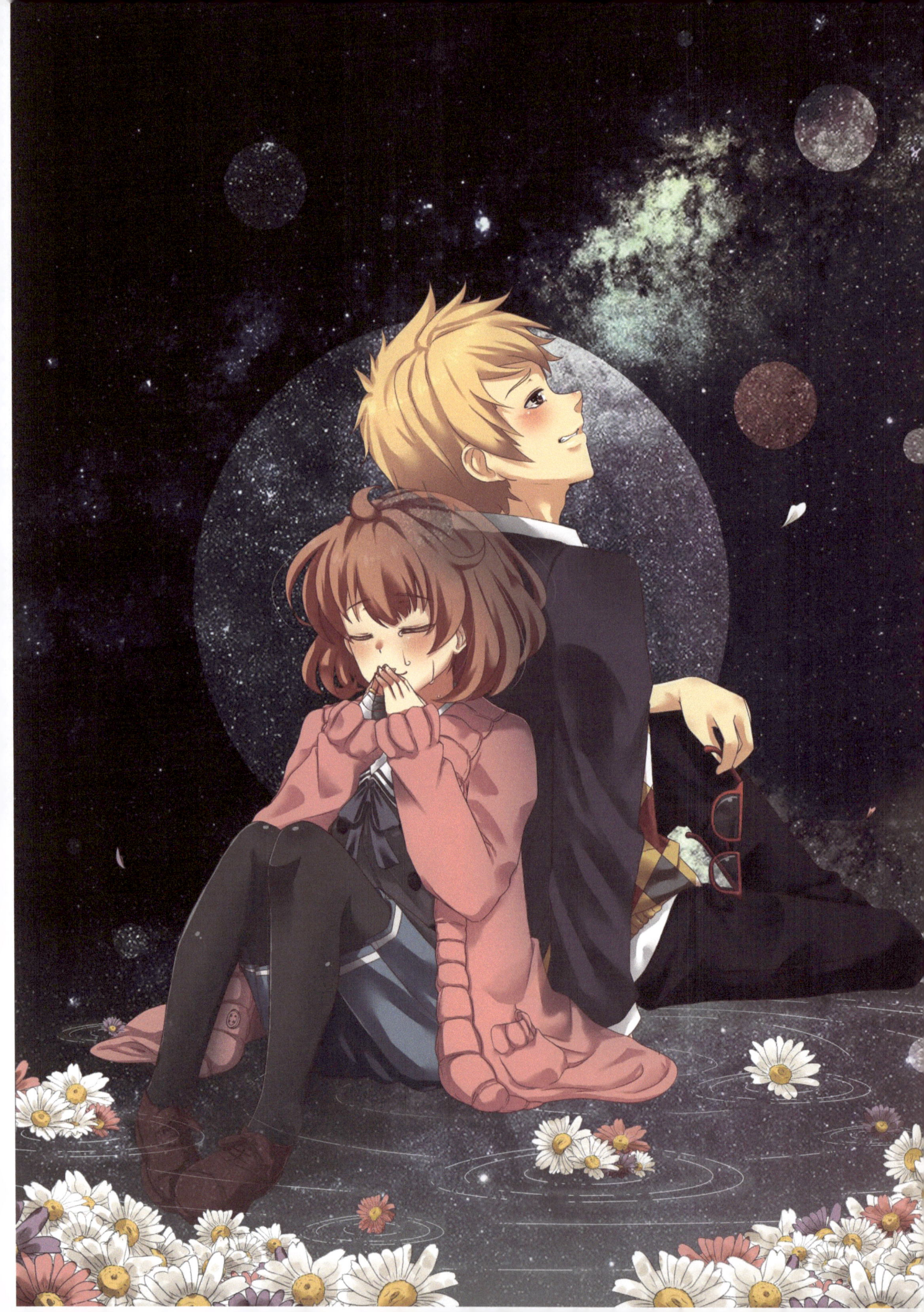

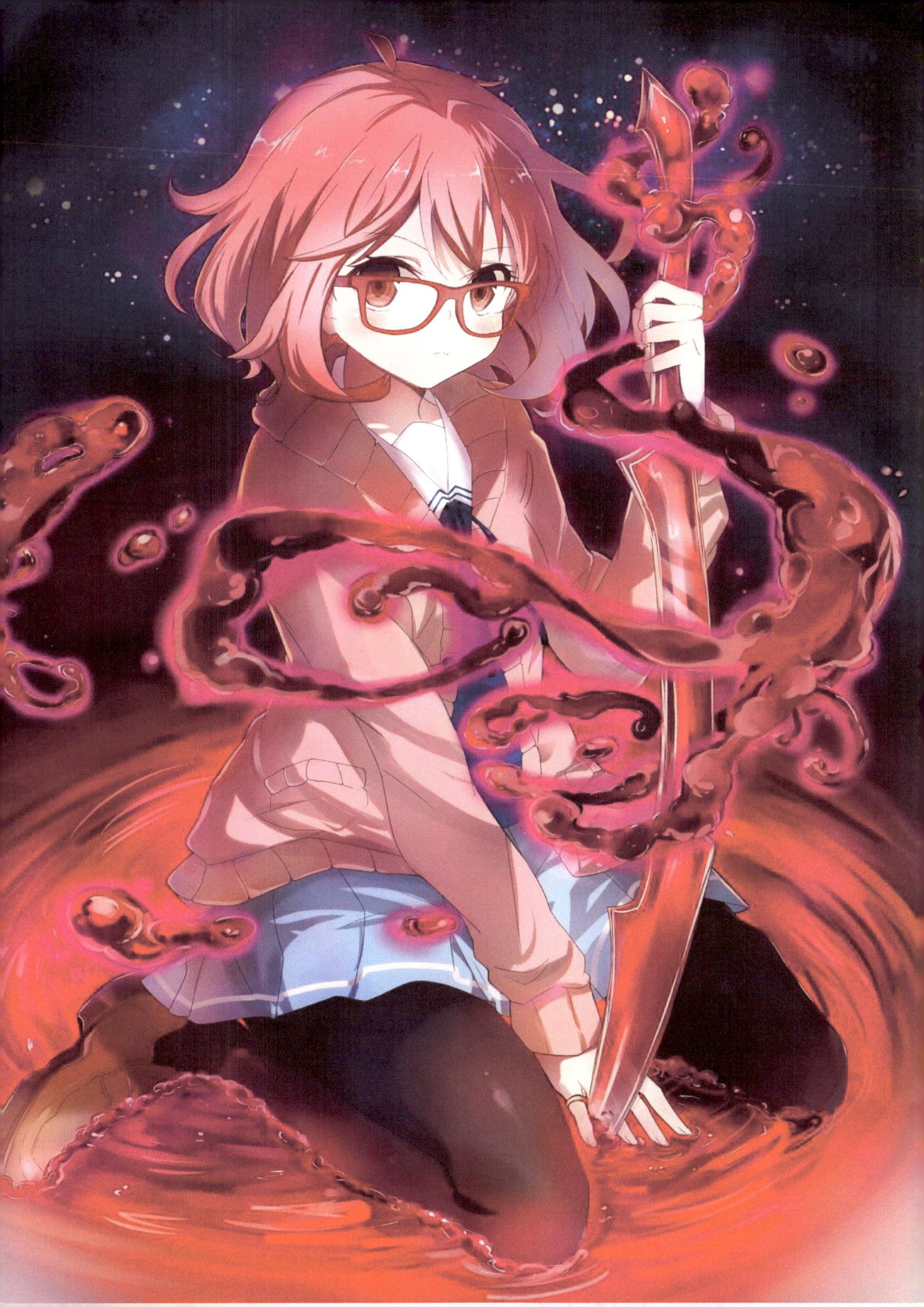

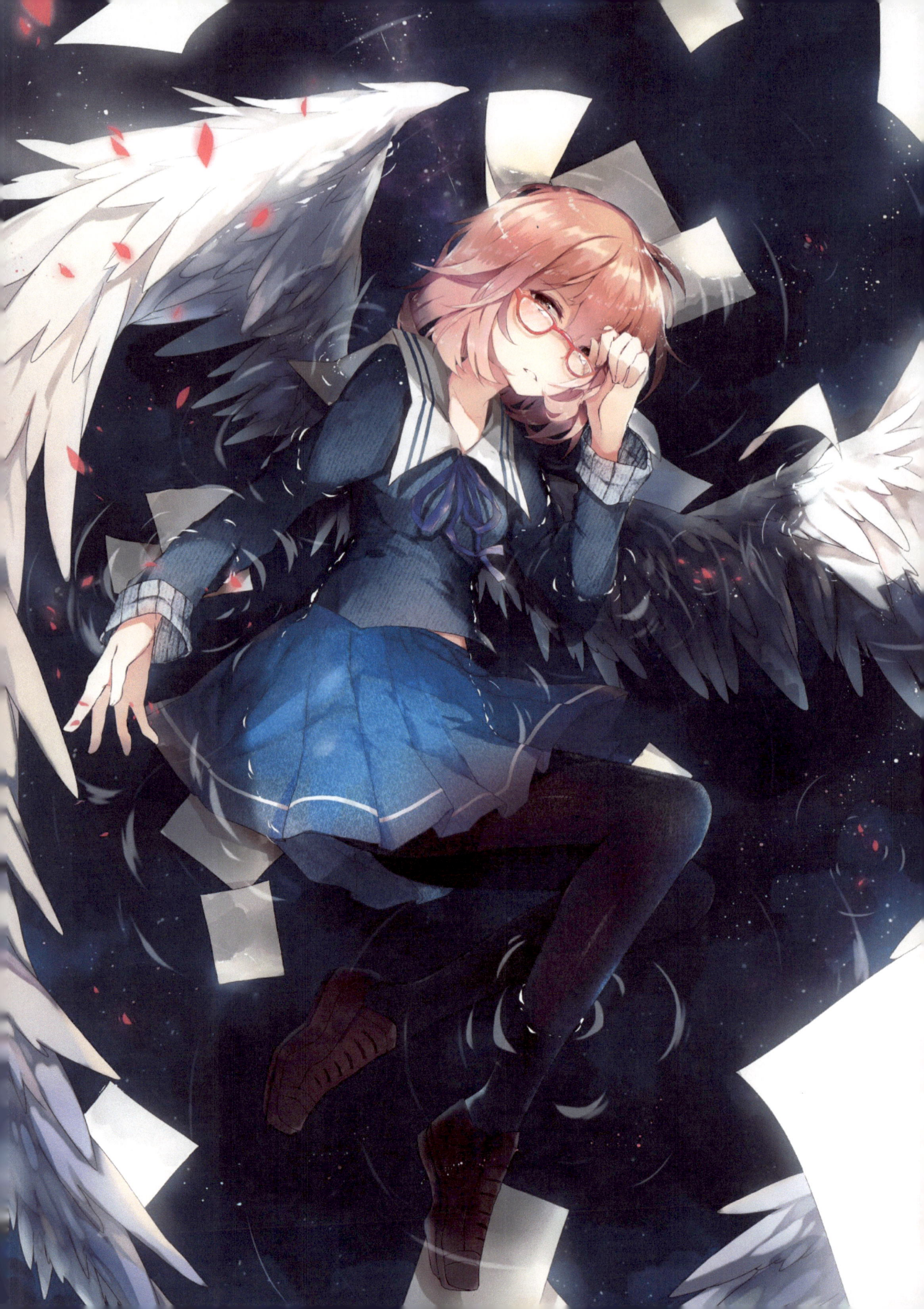

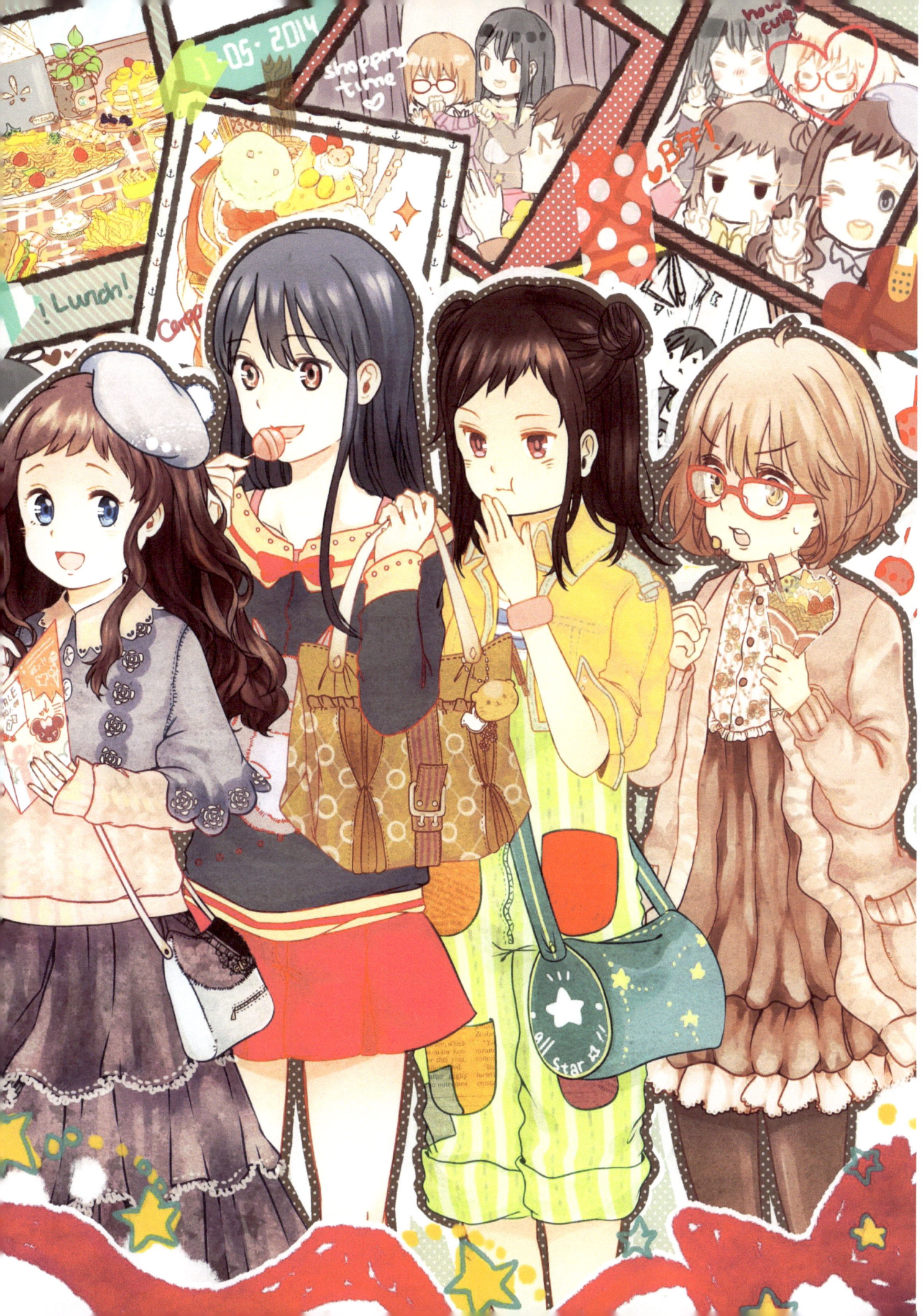

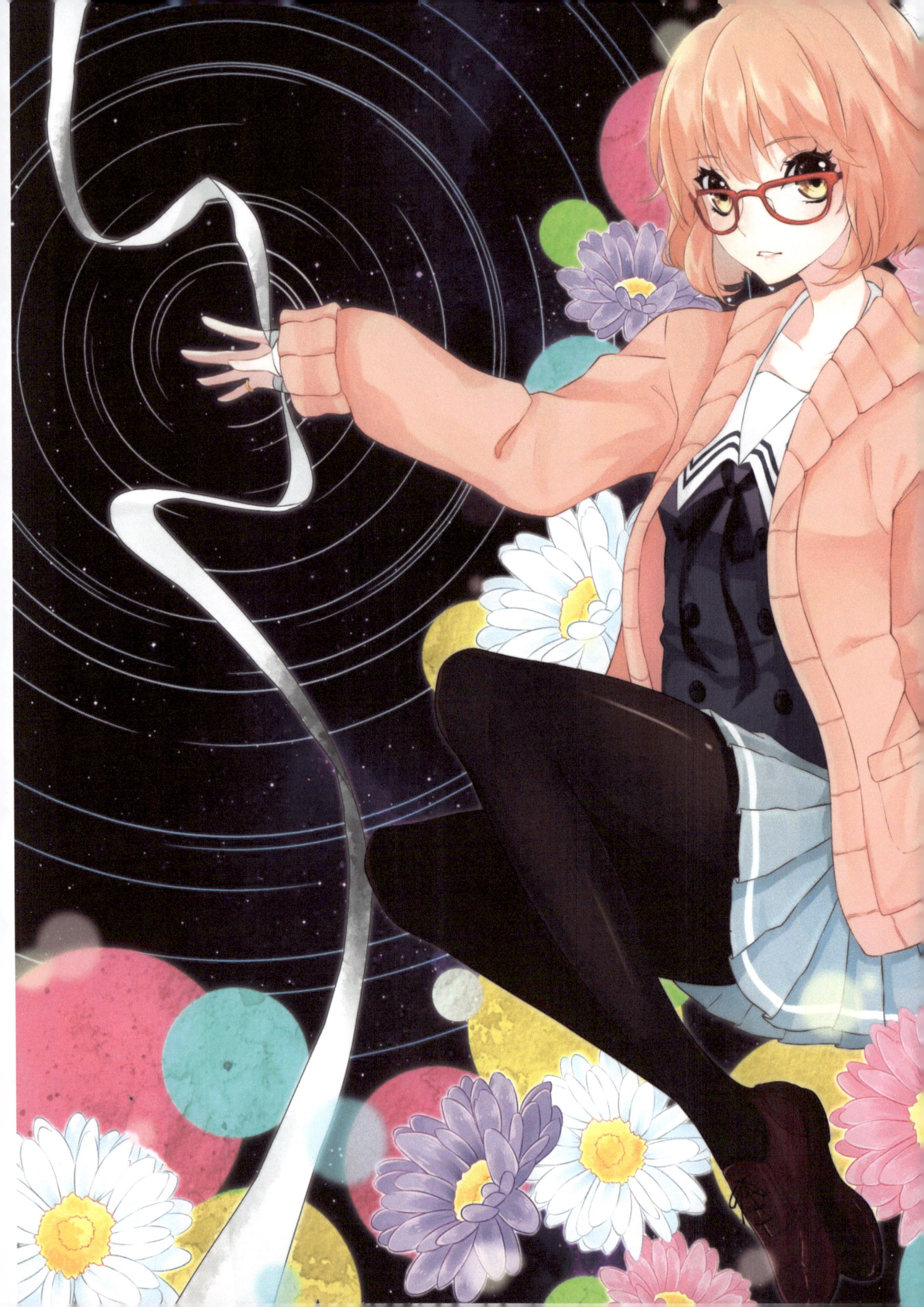

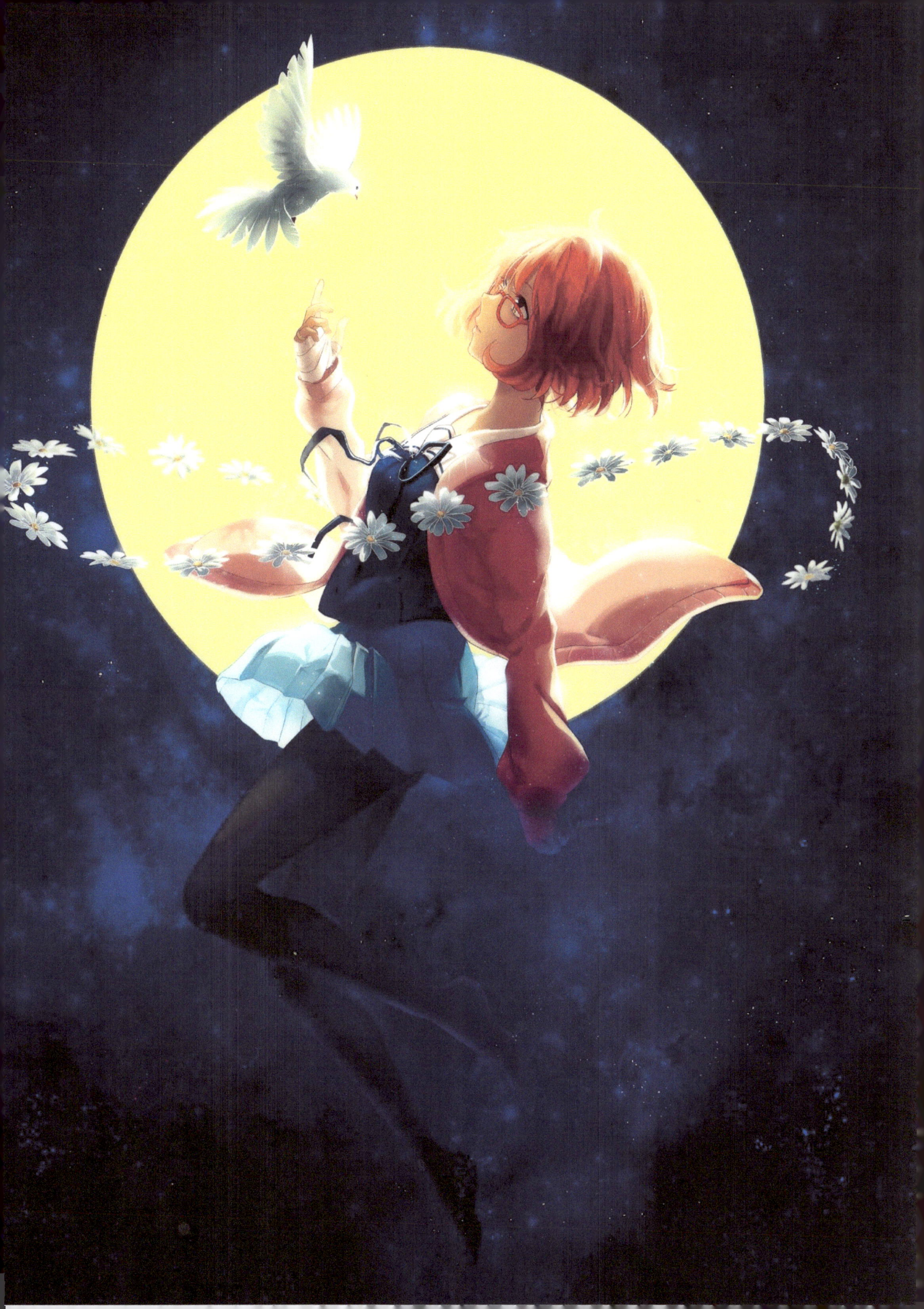

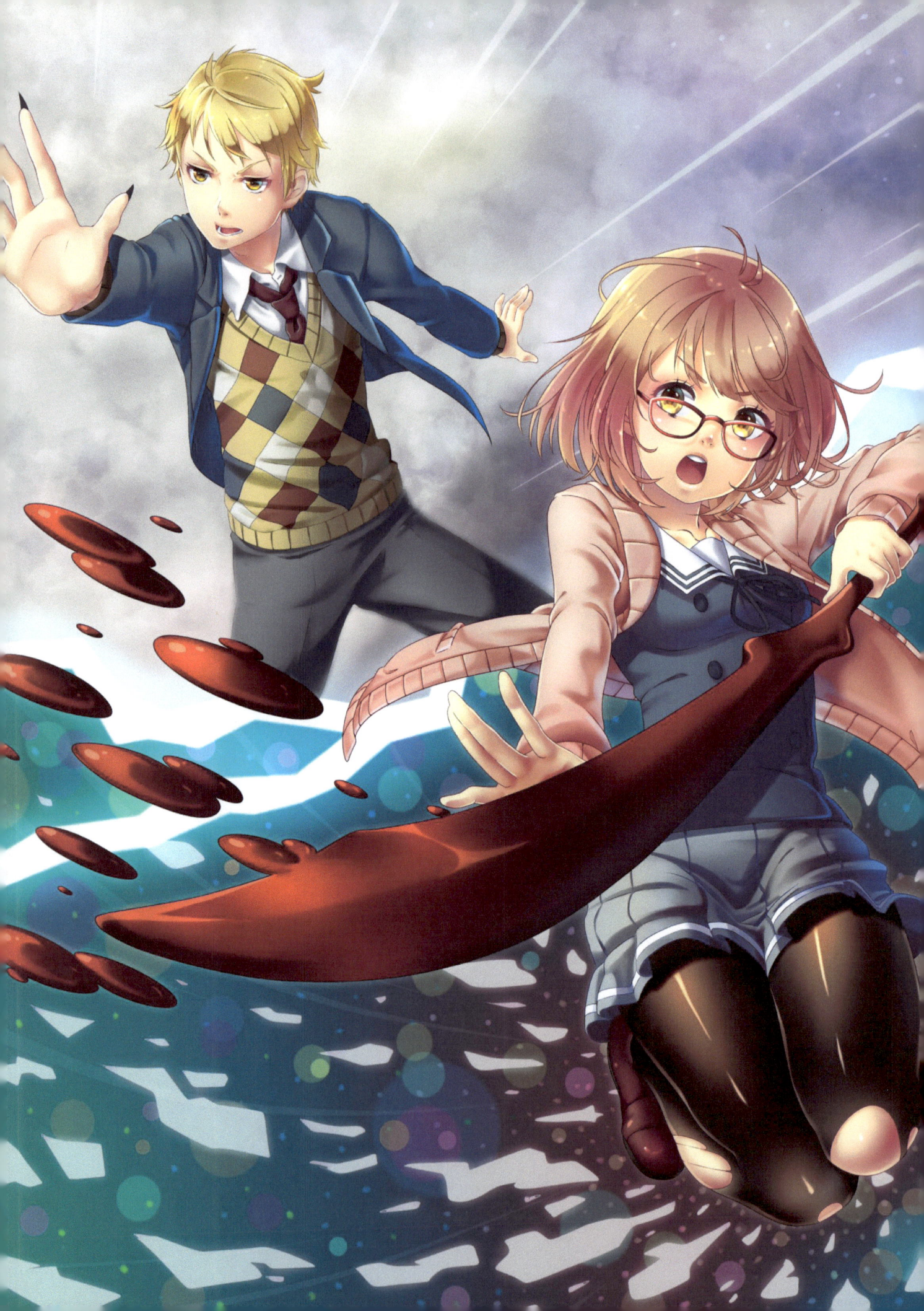

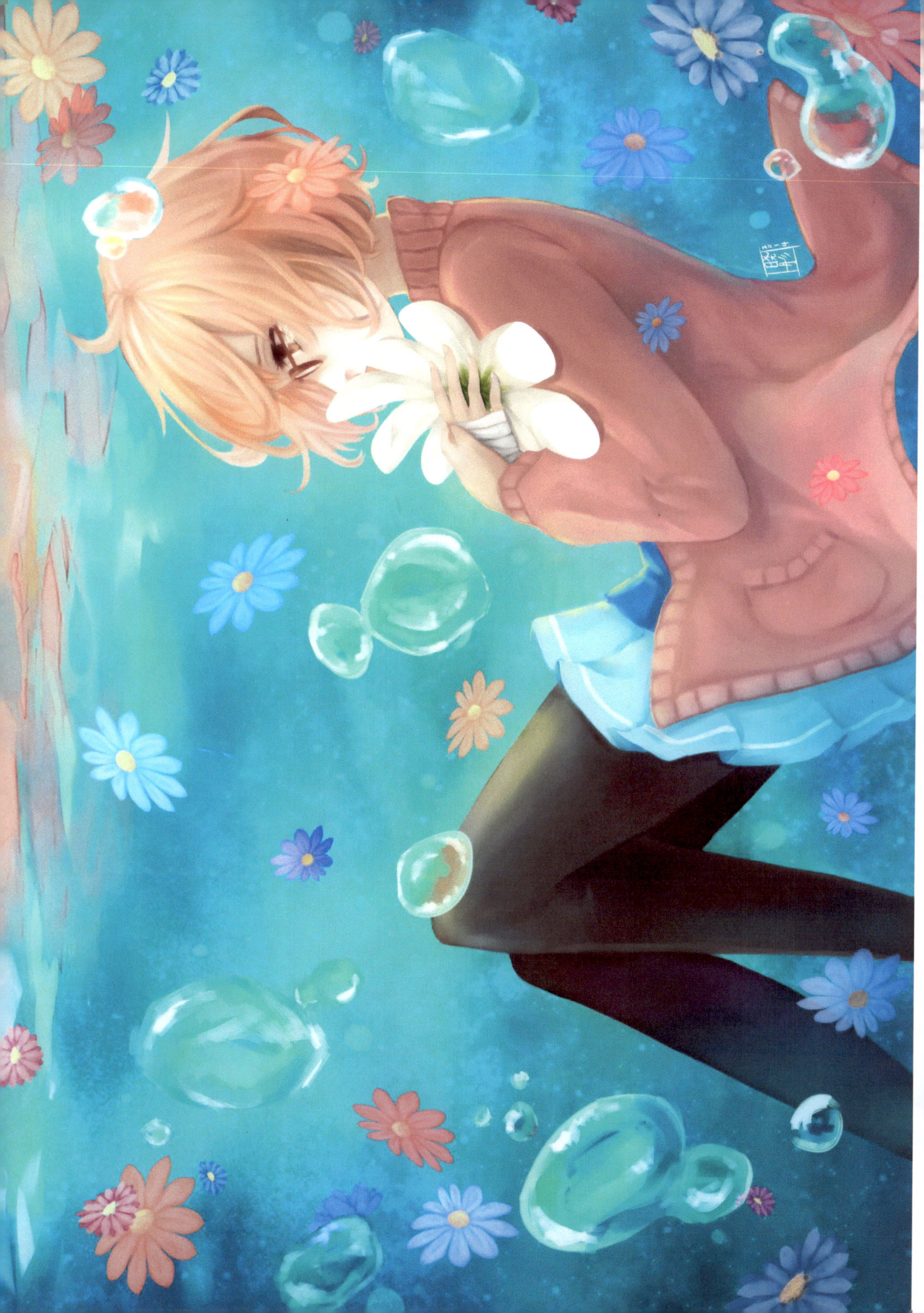

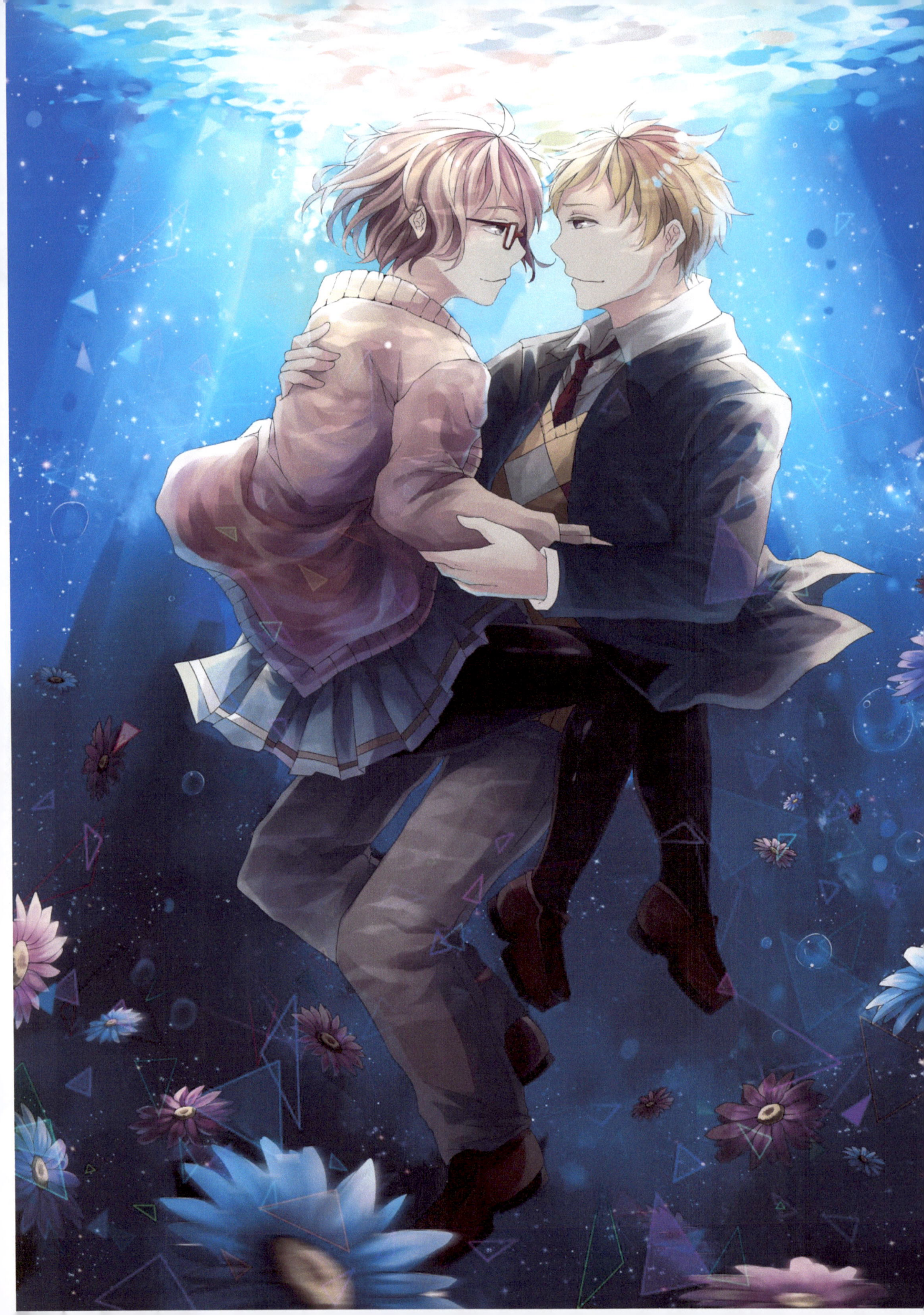

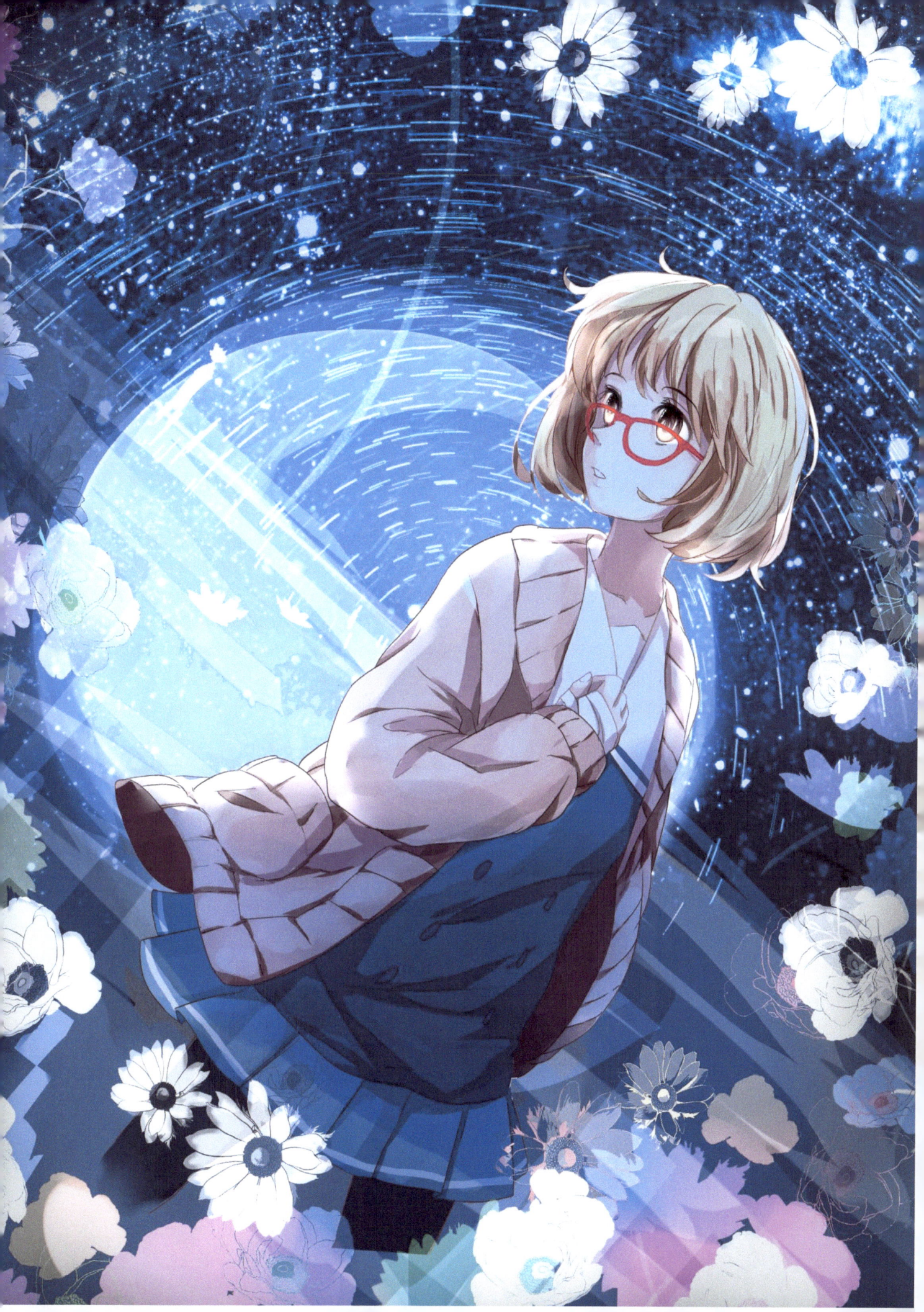

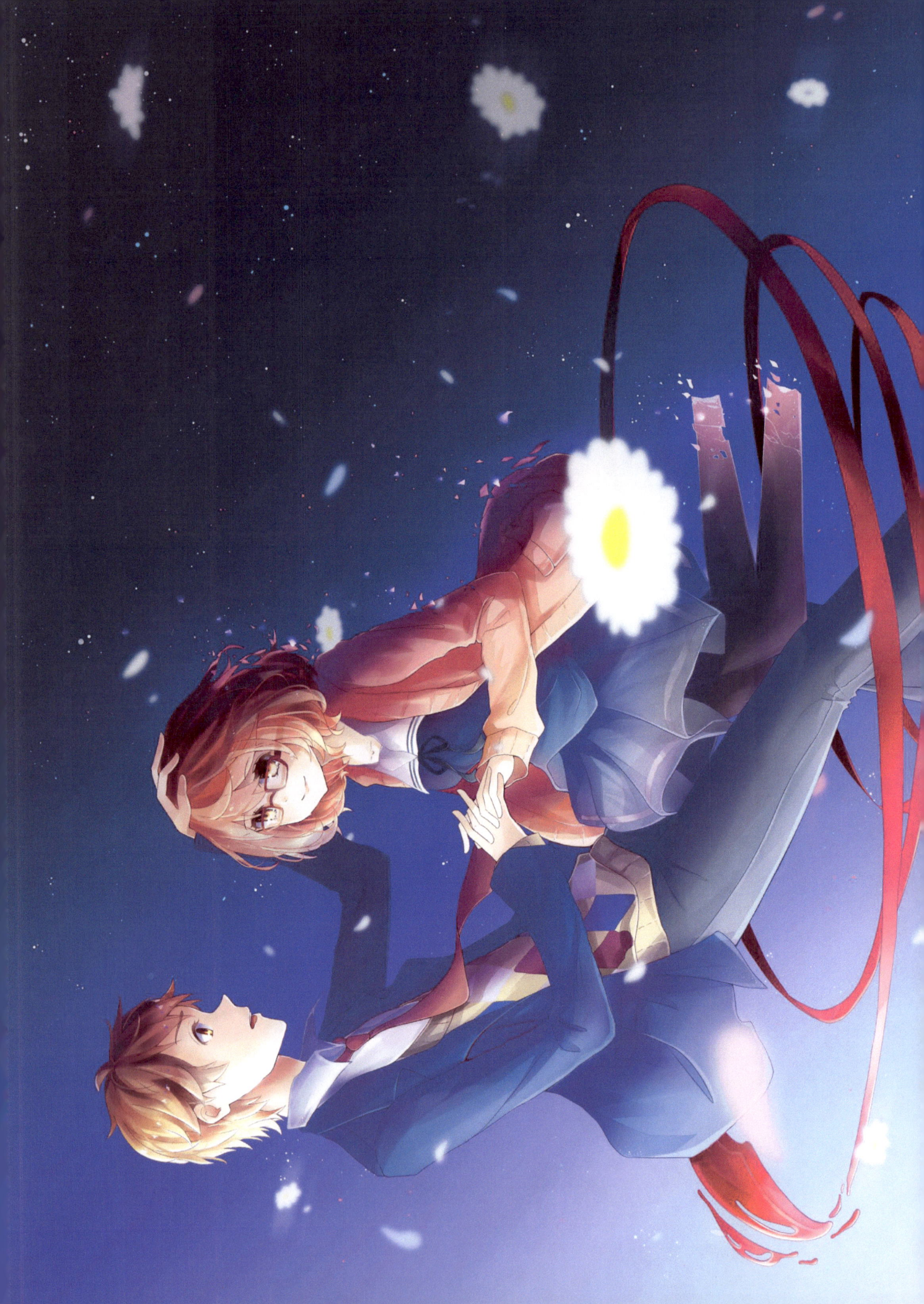

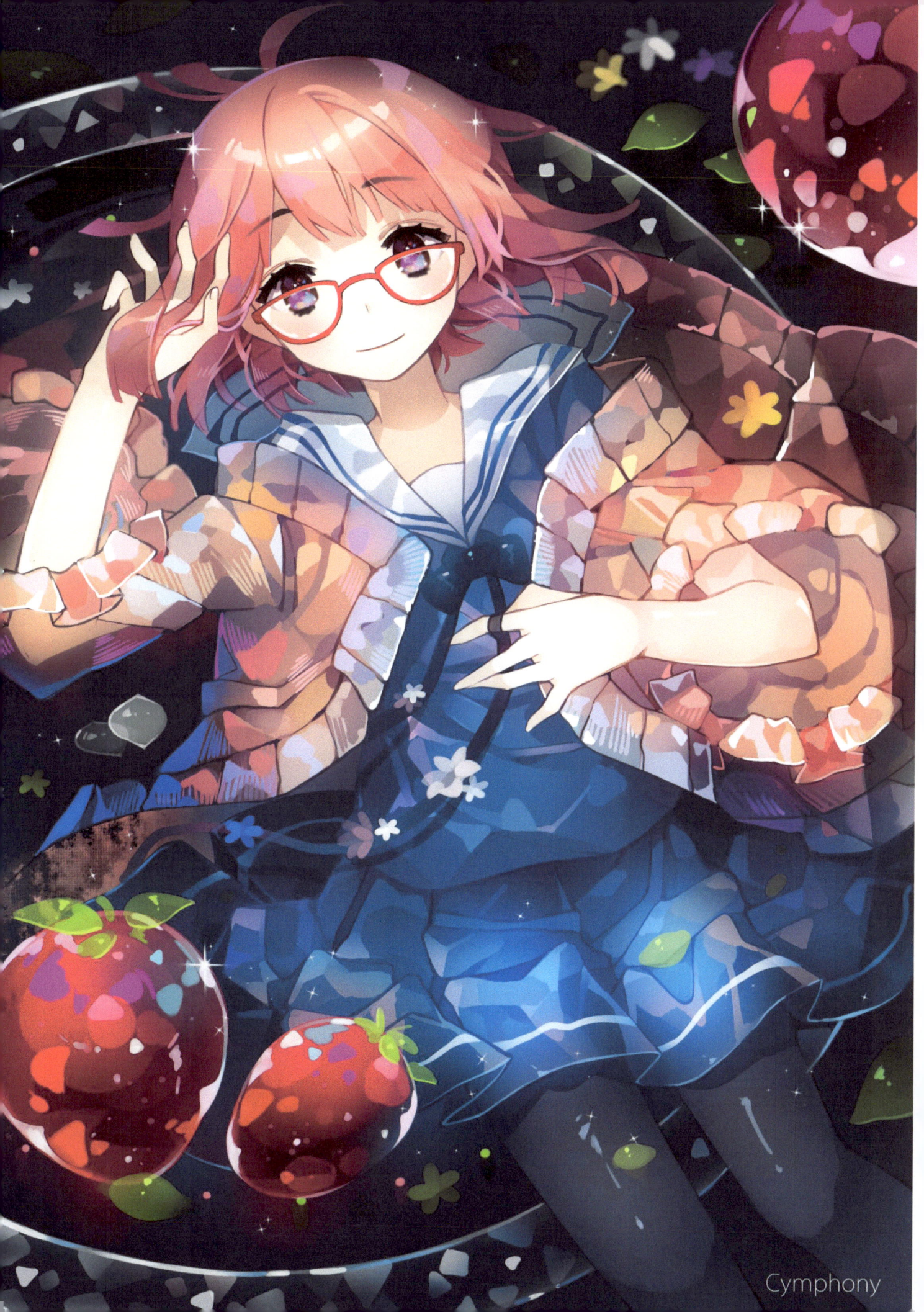

Cymphony

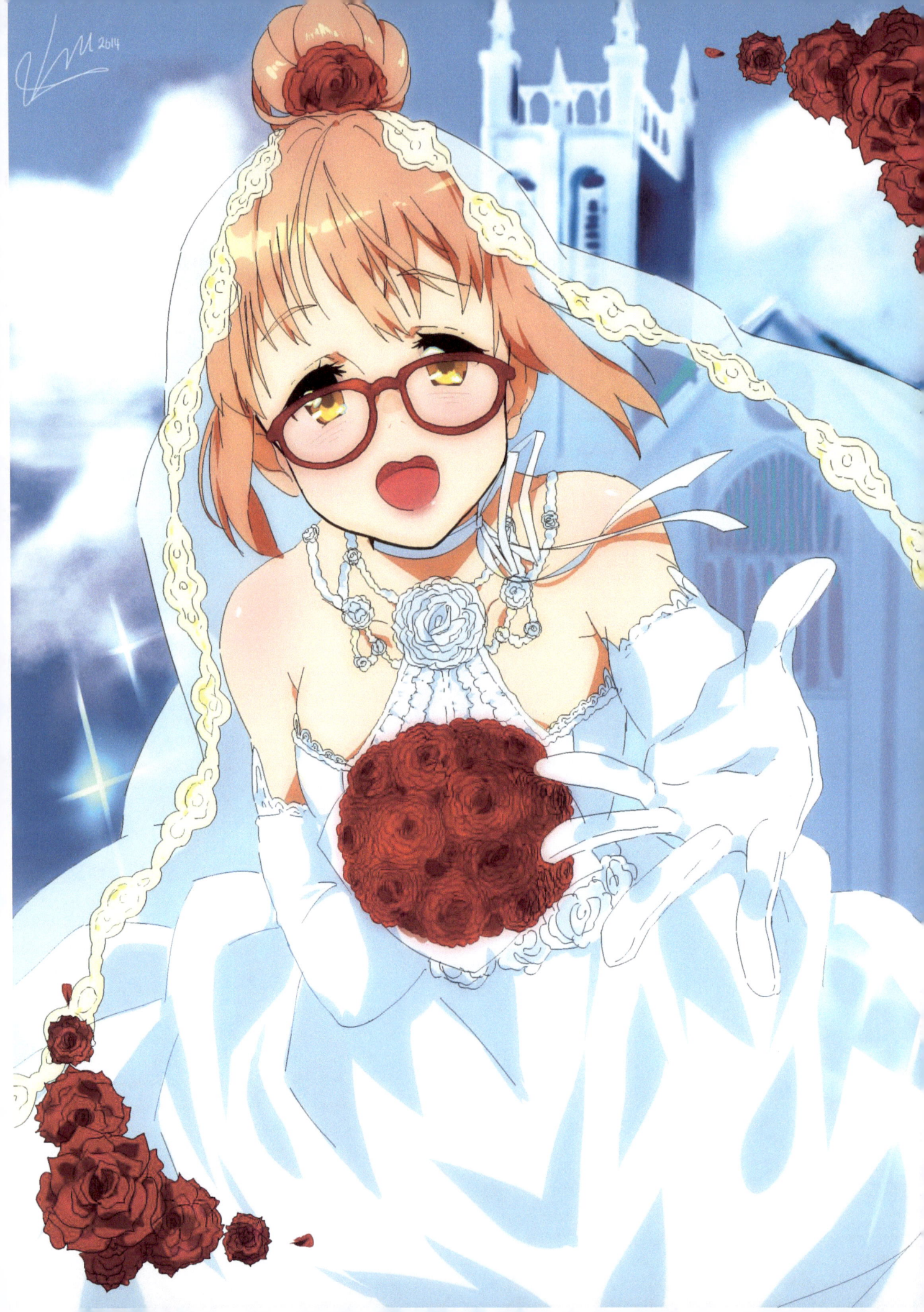

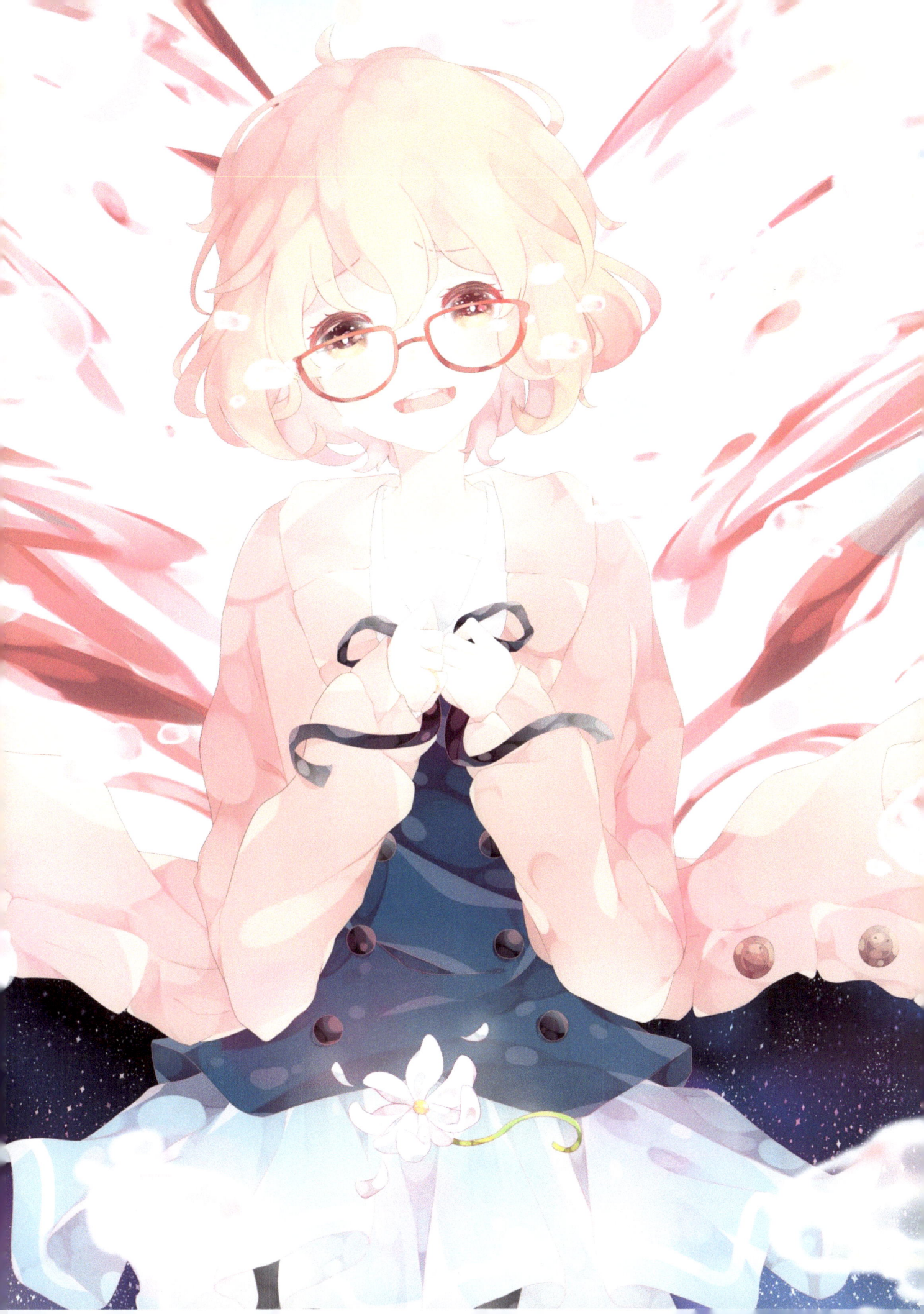

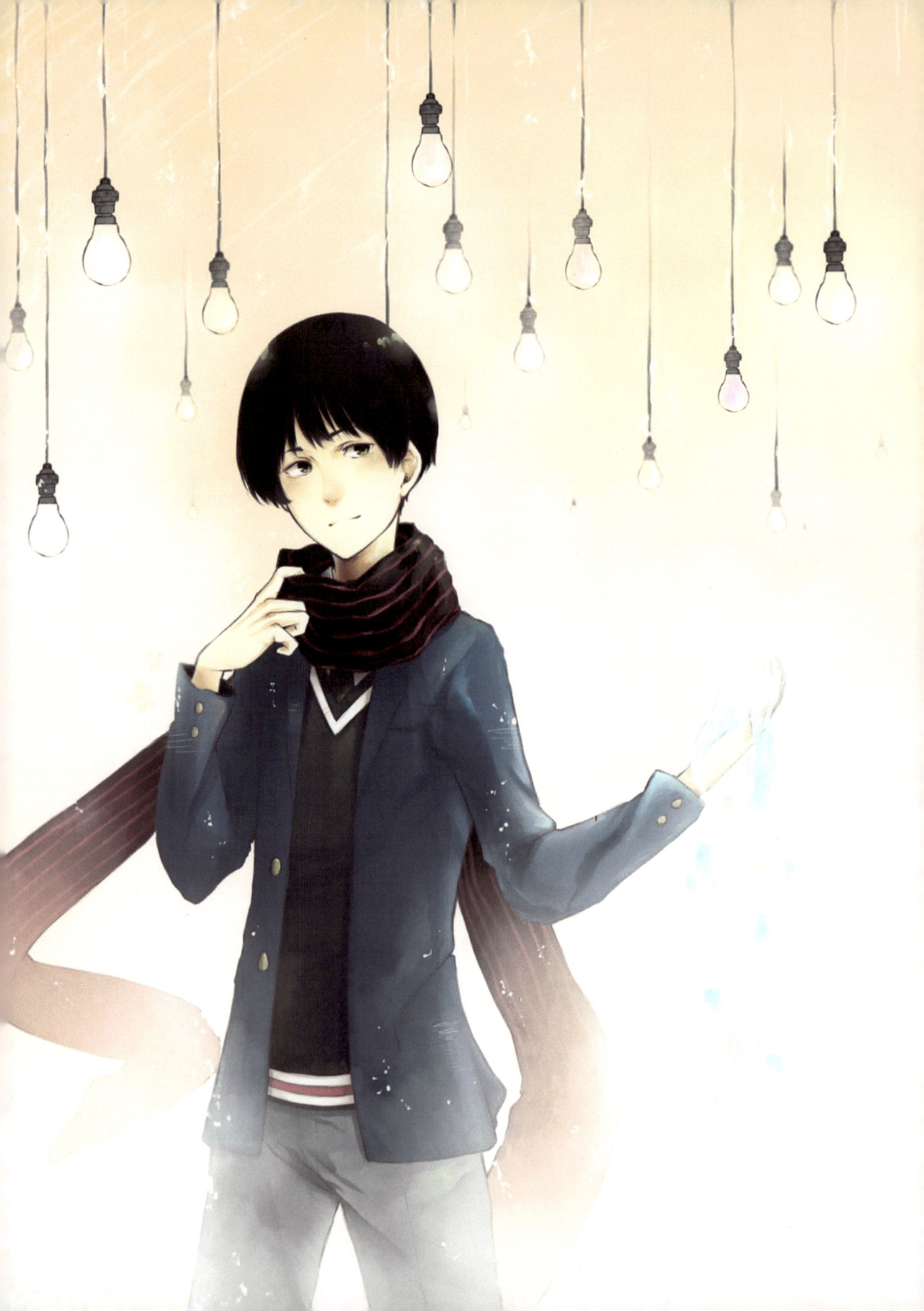

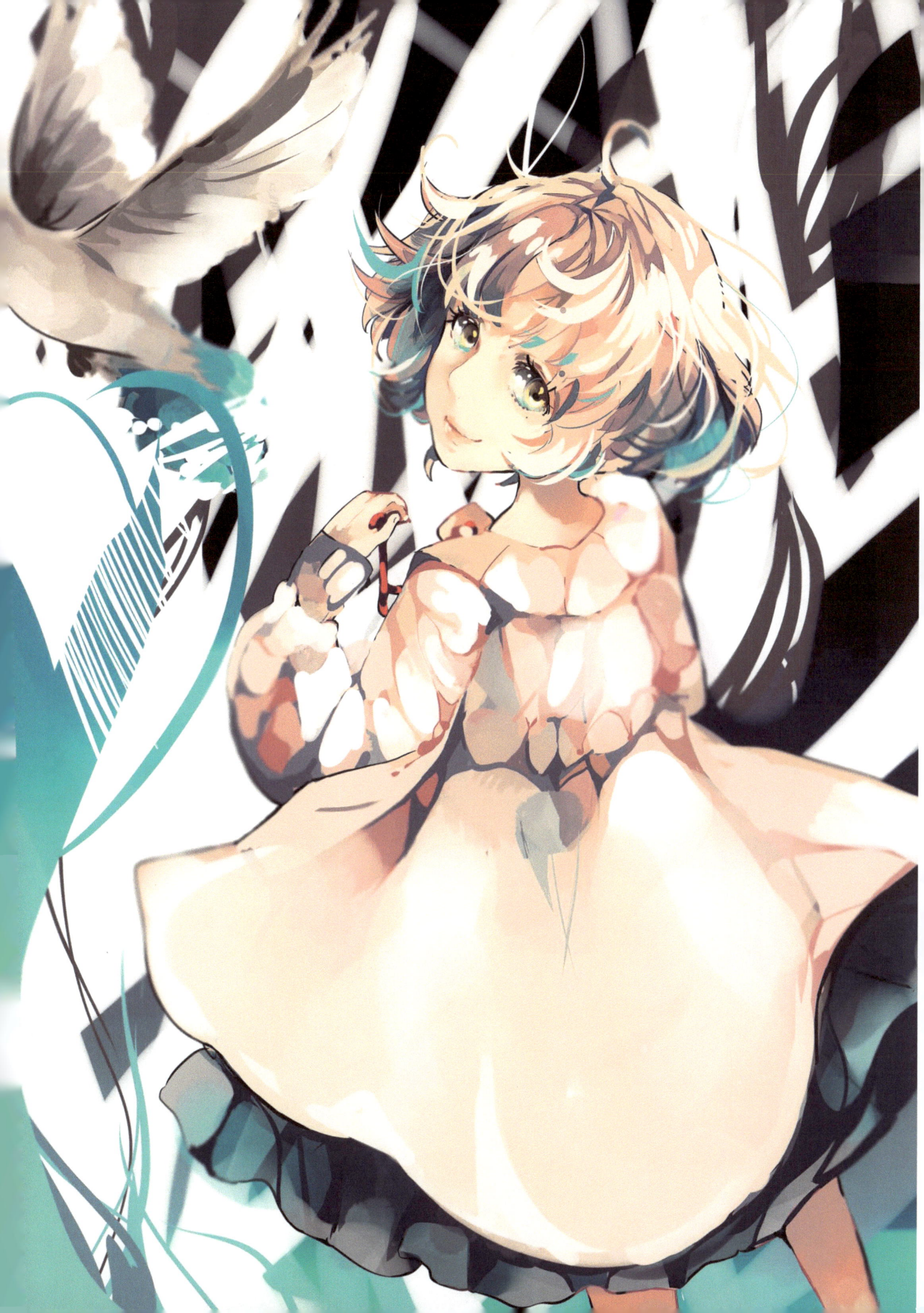

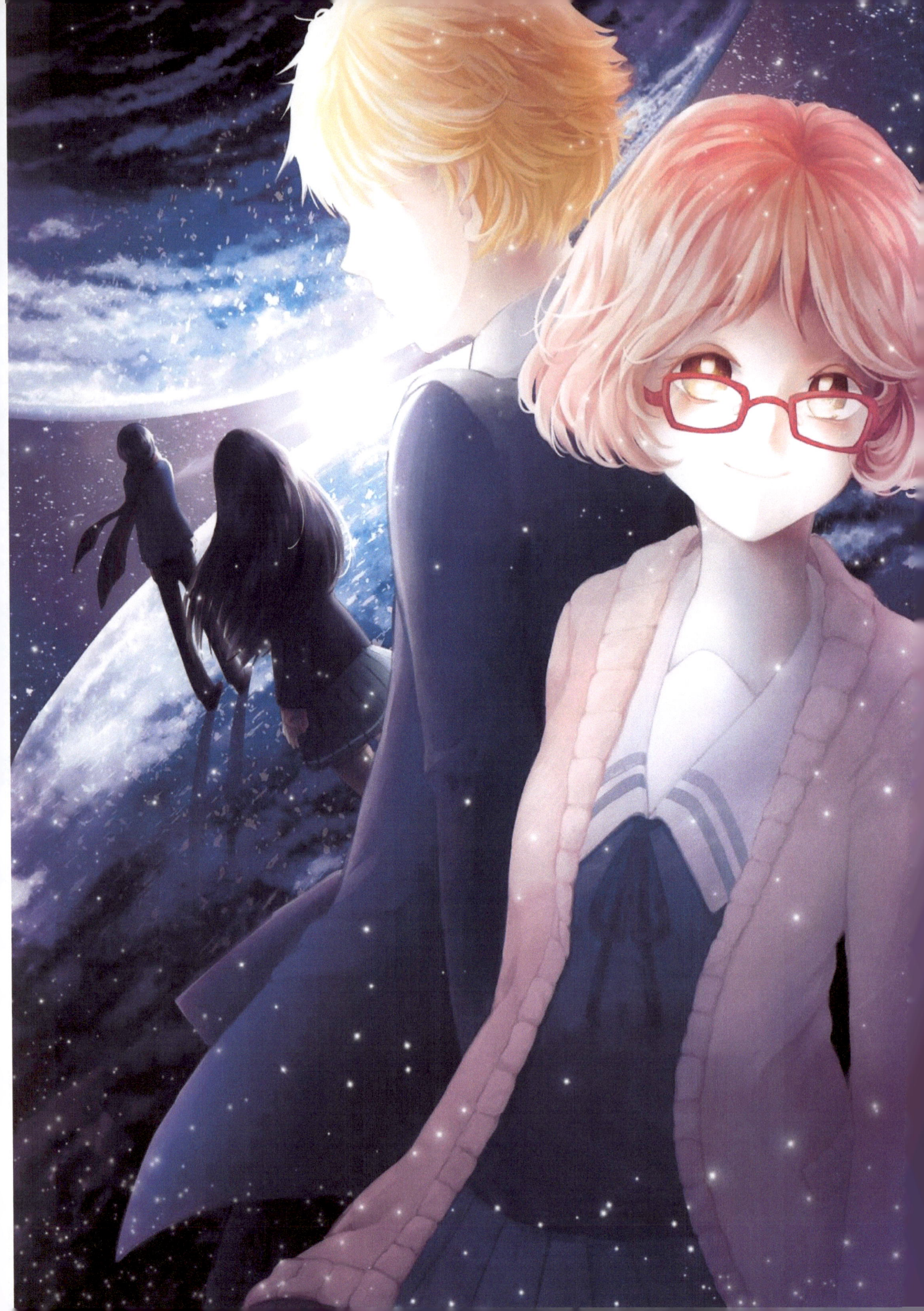

C·R·E·D·I·T·S

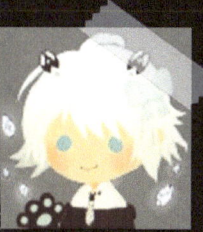
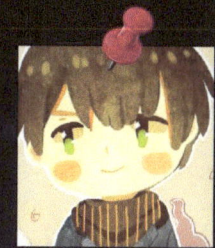

NAME: DOOLI
WEBSITE: HTTP://WWW·DAYRILI·DEVIANTART·COM

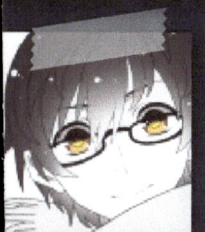
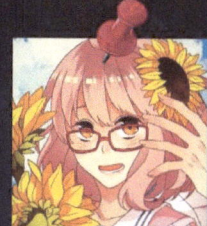

NAME: ELDRIYAN
WEBSITE: HTTP://WWW·ELDRIYAN·DEVIANTART·COM

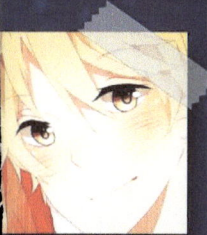
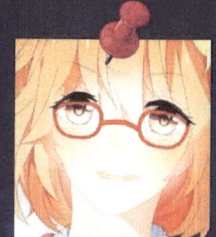

NAME: BURU
WEBSITE: HTTP://WWW·BURU-CHII·DEVIANTART·COM

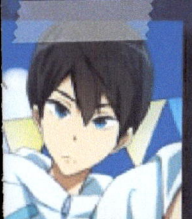
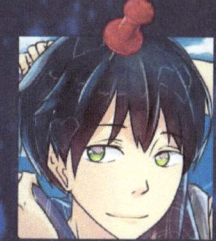

NAME: PIGEON
WEBSITE: HTTP://WWW·HARUKAAAAAAA·TUMBLR·COM/

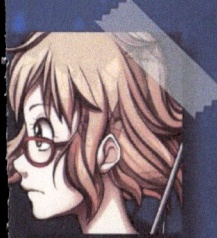
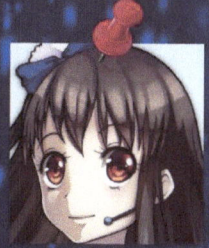

NAME: LAURA ALICE
WEBSITE: HTTP://WWW·LAURA-ALICE-ART·TUMBLR·COM

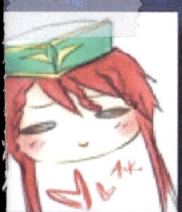
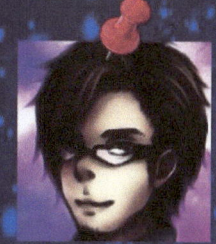

NAME: AI'EURI
WEBSITE: HTTP://WWW·AIKANDII·DEVIANTART·COM

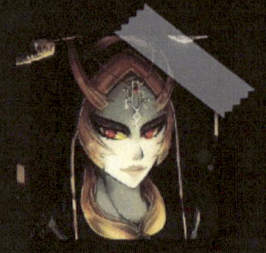
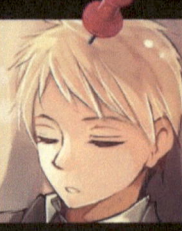

NAME: AO
WEBSITE: HTTP://WWW·ANOKAZUE·DEVIANTART·COM

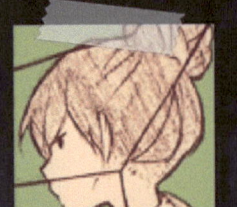
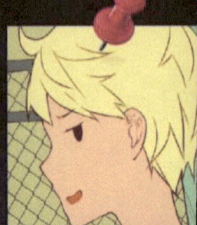

NAME: TOOTOKKI
WEBSITE: HTTP://WWW·TOOTOKKI·TUMBLR·COM

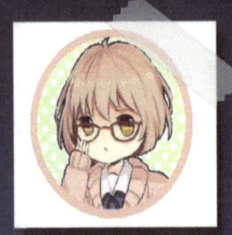
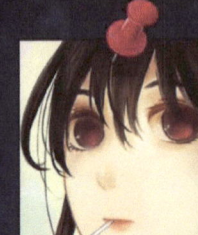

NAME: XIN
WEBSITE: HTTP://WWW·XIN-YII·TUMBLR·COM
COMMENT: MITSUKI IS UNDERAPPRECIATED!

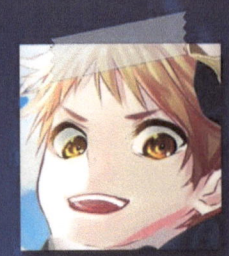
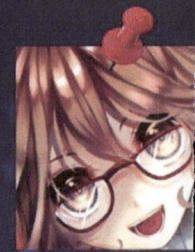

NAME: YAMICCHI
WEBSITE: HTTP://WWW·YAMICCHI·DEVIANTART·COM

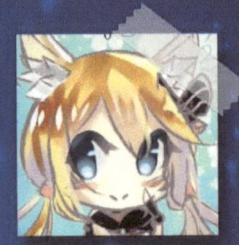
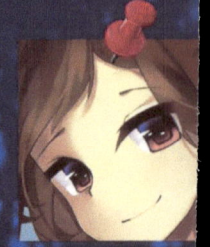

NAME: HIMECHUI
WEBSITE: HTTP://WWW·HIMECHUI·DEVIANTART·COM
COMMENT: Thank you for the guest invite, its an honour to
be a part of this project!!! I hope you enjoy this book >v<

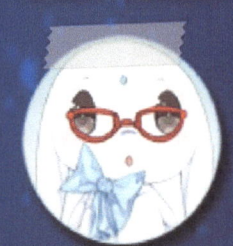
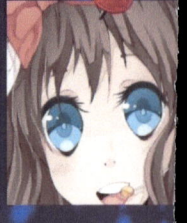

NAME: NYREE R· (EVERGLAVES)
WEBSITE: HTTP://WWW·EVERGLAVES·DEVIANTART·COM
EMAIL: NYREERAINE@HOTMAIL·COM
COMMENT: It is such an honour to be able to participate in
this gorgeous KnK fanbook with so many amazing artists· <3

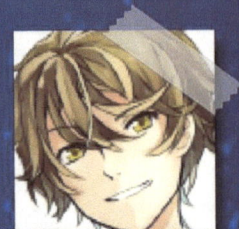
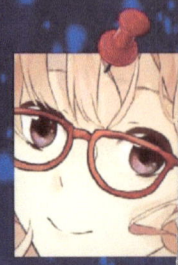

NAME: CLOUDKOURIN
WEBSITE: HTTP://WWW·CLOUDKOURIN·DEVIANTART·COM

Chartreuse L

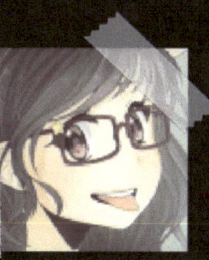

NAME: HARUKATSUNE
WEBSITE: HTTP://WWW·HARUKATSUNE·DEVIANTART·COM
EMAIL: HARUKAY@HOTMAIL·COM

COMMENT: Thank you for the invite! It is truly an honor to
participate in such a beautiful artbook· Also, thank you for working
so hard and diligently to create this artbook!
In other words, I love you, who loves Kyoukai No Kanata··!!

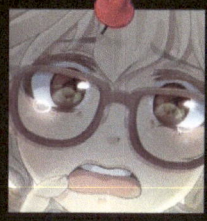

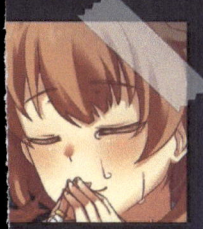

NAME: LIN ALICE HU
WEBSITE: HTTP://WWW·LINHFISH·TUMBLR·COM
CONTACT: LIN·ALICE·HU@GMAIL·COM

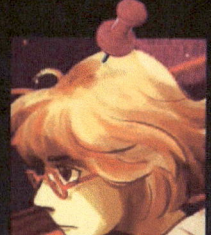

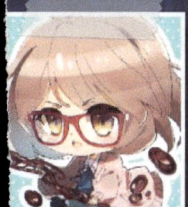

NAME: JENNPADILLO
WEBSITE: HTTP://WWW·JENNPADILLO·DEVIANTART·COM

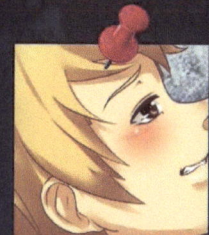

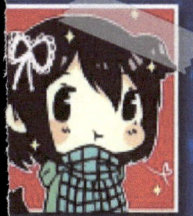

NAME: KAGURA KUROSAKI
WEBSITE: HTTP://WWW·KAGURA-KUROSAKI·DEVIANTART·COM

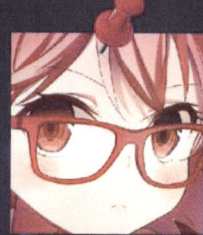

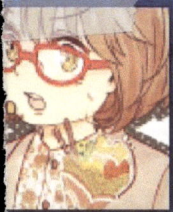

NAME: KANE
WEBSITE: HTTP://WWW·LUKANETA·DEVIANTART·COM
COMMENT: Thank you very much for having me in this book!
It's a great honor to work alongside the rest of the artists~

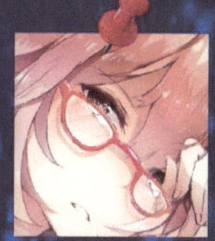

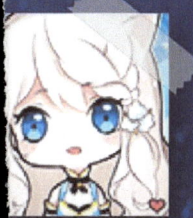

NAME: EVIDAE
WEBSITE: HTTP://WWW·NAOYATOUDO·DEVIANTART·COM
COMMENT: Thank you for having me! Anyway, I just wanna
draw these gals to be happy, so here it is !

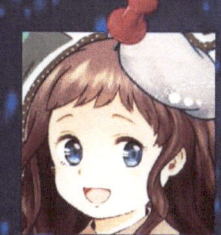

NAME: MOOCHIRIN
WEBSITE: HTTP://WWW·MOOCHIRIN·DEVIANTART·COM
EMAIL: MOOCHIRIN@GMAIL·COM

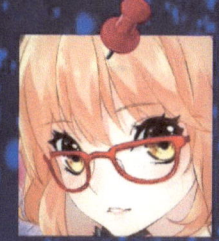

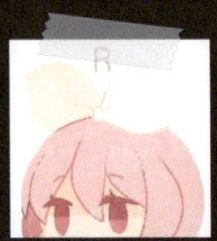
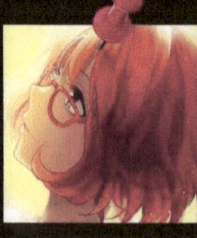

NAME: ROSUURI
WEBSITE: HTTP://WWW·ROSUURI·DEVIANTART·COM
EMAIL: ROSUBERRY@YAHOO·CA

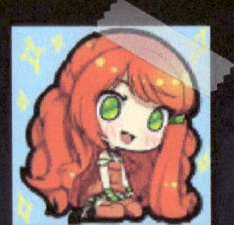
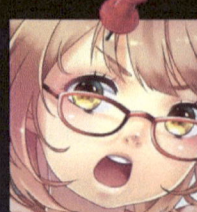

NAME: VALI
WEBSITE: HTTP://WWW·VALI233·DEVIANTART·COM
COMMENT: I'm so happy to be a part of this book~ Please
enjoy!

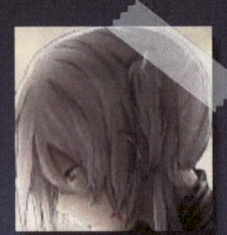
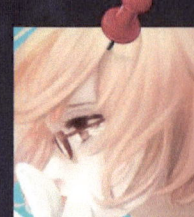

NAME: 曉彤
WEBSITE: HTTP://WWW·NUMILKTEA·TUMBLR·COM

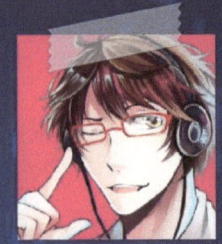
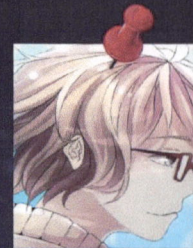

NAME: WARU
WEBSITE: HTTP://WWW·WARUTAICHI·TUMBLR·COM

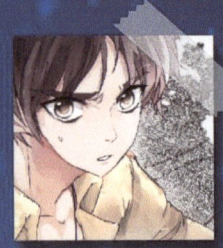
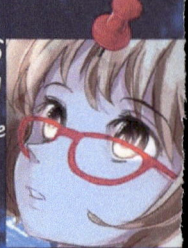

NAME: DUCKIE   PIXIV ID: 1253686
WEBSITE: HTTP://WWW·NODUCKIEALLOW·DEVIANTART·COM
COMMENT: Hi, Everyone! This is Duckie and I wanted to thank Magibubble
for inviting me to be part of this fanbook production· *u* Even though it's
been a long time after Kyoukai no Kanata ended, I still adore these
characters so much! Thank you for purchasing, and I hope you all enjoy this
artbook as much as I do lol!

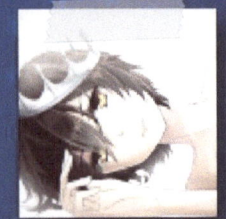
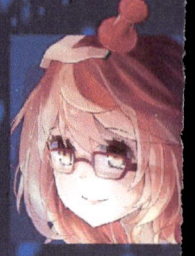

NAME: KUSUREA
WEBSITE: HTTP://WWW·KUSUREA·DEVIANTART·COM
COMMENT: This is my first time participating in an artbook,
thank you very much for the opportunity!

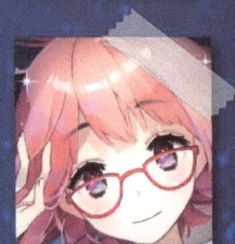
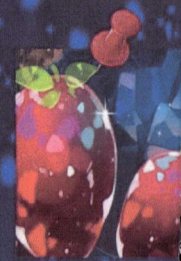

NAME: CYMPHONY
WEBSITE: HTTP://WWW·CYMPHONY·TUMBLR·COM

Chartreuse L

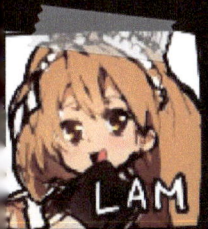

NAME: LILLY MUKO
WEBSITE: HTTP://WWW.LAMCUBED.DEVIANTART.COM

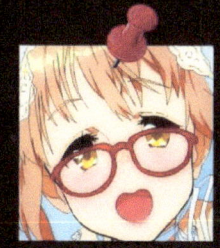

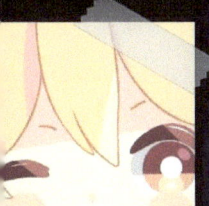

NAME: JOSIE
WEBSITE: HTTP://WWW.MEI-MI.DEVIANTART.COM

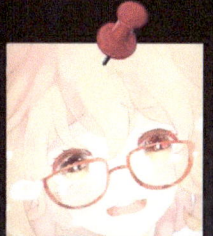

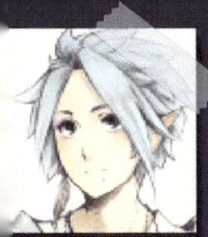

NAME: ZERA
WEBSITE: HTTP://WWW.ZERAFIA.TUMBLR.COM
COMMENT: I'm really happy that I got to work with all these
artists, thank you for asking me in this project! ;v;

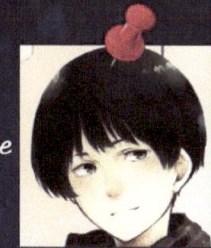

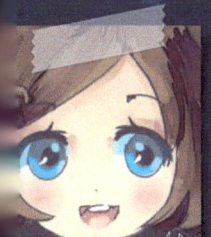

NAME: KYOUKARAA
WEBSITE: HTTP://WWW.KYOUKARAA.DEVIANTART.COM

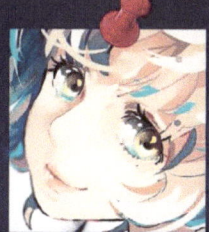

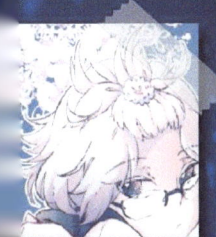

NAME: 'toumin'   PIXIV ID: 1931104
WEBSITE: HTTP://WWW.TOUMIN.DEVIANTART.COM
            HTTP://WWW.TOUMIN.TUMBLR.COM

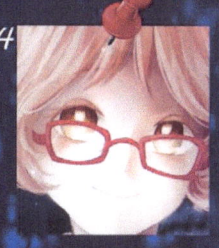

Thank you to all the talented Guest Artists that participated in
Chartreuse Light - this book wouldn't have been the same without
each and every one of you!

I hope everyone enjoys this book and the wonderful art that the
Artists have submitted - it's amazing to see such a wide variety
of different styles.

Make sure to check out the links from the Guest Artists
throughout these final pages if you'd like to see more of their
wonderful work!

-Magi

Chartreuse Light